A God to Glorify
Notes on being a Parish Minister

Frederick Levison (1910-1999) was a parish minister in the Church of Scotland for over forty years, followed by twelve years in the pew. He has written *The Gospel at Infant Baptism*; *Christian and Jew: Leon Levison 1881-1936*, an account of his father's life; and *The Prospect of Heaven: Musings of an enquiring believer*.

A God to Glorify

Notes on being a Parish Minister

Frederick Levison

St Bernard Press
Gifford, Scotland

Published by
St Bernard Press
The Manse
Tweeddale Avenue
Gifford
Haddington EH41 4QN
Scotland

First published 2000

Distributed in New Zealand by
Archdeacon R.J. Nicholson
29 Radiata Street
Hamilton

Distributed in the United States of America by
First Presbyterian Church
709 South Boston Avenue
Tulsa, OK 74119-1629

British Library Cataloguing in Publication Data
Data available

ISBN 0-9538817-0-9

Printed in Great Britain by
Redwood Books Limited
Kennet Way, Trowbridge
Wiltshire BA14 8RN

A Charge to keep I have,
A God to glorify

Charles Wesley

Preface

The manuscript of this book, written in his retirement by Fred Levison around 1982-85, was prepared for publication on his death in 1999 by his wife, Mary, with the help, which is here very gratefully acknowledged, of John O'Neill. In the early 80s inclusive language was not universally used. Please accept that all references to ministers as *he* refer to both men and women. It has been thought best to leave as originally written some expressions which may now be out-of-date, e.g. *Book of Common Order*. The full manuscript has been lodged in the New College Library, University of Edinburgh.

Fred's hope would be that his experiences—both positive and negative—might give some encouragement and help to those starting out on this great calling.

We acknowledge the gracious permission of Macmillan, publishers of Charles Causely, *Collected Poems 1951-2000*, to quote from 'Ten Types of Hospital Visitor.'

We are grateful to the Drummond Trust, 3 Pitt Terrace, Stirling for a grant towards the publication of this book.

M.I.L.

Contents

Part I	*The Scene, the Minister, and the Parish*	
1	Change—and Continuity	1
2	The Man or Woman for the Job	2
3	Finding a Parish	6
Interlude	*'A Bag of Needments' (Chaucer)*	8
Part II	*Worship and Sacraments*	
4	'Let us Worship God'	11
5	Facing the Music	19
6	Preaching: A Joyful Agony	23
7	Baptizing Babies	35
8	Preparing Communicants	43
9	'O Taste and See'	47
Part III	*Pastoralia*	
10	Getting to Know You	50
11	Bedside Manners	61
12	Binding the Brokenhearted	63
13	'To Love and to Cherish'	67
14	'A meeting will be held...'	73
Part IV	*The Flock*	
15	Fostering Fellowship	76
16	Fellow Workers	82
17	Among the Children	86
18	Teenagers—Oh, Help!	88
19	The Parish Pump, and Beyond	93
Part V	*And Furthermore*	
20	Also on the Agenda	97
21	Vocational Hazards	104
Part VI	*A Charge to Keep*	
22	Taking the Strain	110
23	Time to Breathe	114
24	A Charge to Keep	116

Part I
THE SCENE, THE MINISTER, AND THE PARISH

1 Change—and Continuity

Amid all change the basic tasks of the parish minister remain the same. To proclaim Christ and the things of Christ; and to strike the indispensable notes of worship: adoration and thanksgiving, confession and supplication, dedication and intercession. The technique of preaching may be different but the content cannot be other than the Gospel in all its aspects; which entails the elucidation of the Scriptures, the clarifying of the great doctrines, and the presentation in modern terms of the same message that St Paul and St Francis, Luther and Wesley, Spurgeon and Temple, in their different ways, proclaimed.

And as the human heart, with its joys and sorrows, its temptations and doubts, its loving and its sinning, is constant, the pastoral ministry requires not only the latest psychological insights but the spiritual and human gifts it has always needed.

2 The Man or Woman for the Job

The lines were crossed. He rang, and got the wrong number. He rang again. And again. This time he recognised my voice. 'Oh God,' he cried, 'it's the bloody padre!' We commiserated about the telephone services, then he said 'Look here, padre, the hunt is starting from my place at nine tomorrow'—we lived in Berwickshire—'bring your wife along for a drink, or a coffee, and see them off.' For three reasons (a minister's brain always clicks in threes!) that conversation pleased me. First because he didn't apologise for swearing, as if I belonged to an odd species which required special treatment. Second because I like the word *padre*. And third because the offer of coffee hinted that, unlike the apostles at Pentecost, we were not accounted so sybaritic as to indulge at nine in the morning.

He was an ex-Army man still known, thirty years on, as Major. Which is why he said *padre*, a word which is pretty dated outside Army circles. Being a male word it may become obsolete. Perhaps it will soon be old-hat enough to acquire a patina , like a vintage car. In spite of this it is a good word, which in several ways characterises the parish minister as I like to think of him.

Let me explain. In the Services the official word is *chaplain*. It signifies someone assigned a specific role and rank by the establishment—a three pipper on a two pip pay. The padre is the same man without the spit and polish. Seen not as a professional or an official, not even as a priest, but just as a friendly man of God; a bloke who wears a dog-collar, and a cross on his badge to show that his trade is Christianity. And I covet this kind of informality.

The word also implies, and the idea lingers, that he is a father-figure, a father being someone you can disagree with but who is concerned about you, and to whom you can turn in time of need. It is also relevant that in many countries the word *padre* is the equivalent of parish Priest: it has, like *minister*, a community connotation. (In the military context this sense of being a community man is evident; the regimental padre ministering not merely to the few confessing Christians but to all ranks.)

So I relish the word; but no less do I love the title *minister*. There can be no greater appellation for it is used of Him who came 'not to be ministered unto but to minister.' We have come more and more to see it, however, as a word we cannot keep to ourselves in the profession. Every Christian has a ministry to perform, and ministry has many forms. The ministry of Word and Sacrament performed in a parochial setting is but one of these. An essential one and vital to the Church's future, although the parish minister is 'not the whole cheese'. But since parish minister rings bells which parish padre, except for a few of us, would not set a-tolling, it is the title to which I shall adhere.

As for the essentials of a job-description, you could ponder St Paul's words in Ephesians 4. 'As God has called you, live up to your calling. Be humble always and gentle, and patient too. Be forbearing with one another and charitable. Spare no effort to make fast with bonds of peace the unity which the Spirit gives.'

The Call

I dallied until my final university year before becoming a candidate. Deeply attached to the Church I had for long wanted to be a minister and I had been nudged towards it by a score of Christian influences—but was I really called? In those days there were no selection schools. But when, having taken the plunge, I arrived at the divinity college I discovered that our first task was to write a paper for the Principal on 'My Call to the Ministry', in the light of which he would interview us one by one. It was a test which shattered one of my fellow-students who, after a painful self-scrutiny, disappeared—to surface at the College of Education.

I had no mystic call or palpable vision. What enabled me to line up decisively as a candidate were two truths culled from my reading, and which were the basis of my paper. The first was simply the phrase 'faith is interpretation'; the second that 'the world's need may be God's call to you'. Thus I was able to interpret the many signposts pointing me to the ministry as the finger of God; and the patent need of the world for the Church, and the Church for ordained ministers, as His call. Had I known them then, I would surely also have responded to Henry Drummond's words to an enquirer who wanted some sign from God: 'Look for no other sign than an increasing readiness to do His will.'

Self doubt springs from self knowledge as well as from confusion about vocation. Who is sufficient for these things? It is a holy calling and like Isaiah we are men of unclean lips. Also, many of us are not highly endowed. We do not have the commanding presence

3

and the compelling tongue of the great preachers nor the incisive scholarly mind; we may be shy by nature and not great mixers; diffident too, in leadership; neither sharp-witted nor bubbling with *joie de vivre*; better with men than women, or *vice versa*, awkward, perhaps, with children. Yet we cannot be all that bad or the selection boards would not let through so many who are like us. The root of the matter must be there or they, and we, would be turned away.

The miracle is this. That through the years, by God's grace and the working of the Holy Spirit, many seemingly mediocre and colourless candidates blossom until their influence is like that of Joseph whom the scriptures compare to 'a fruitful bough, even a bough by a well, whose branches run over the wall'. And a part of our calling, need it be said, is to live close by that well.

A communicator of the gospel

Since our business is communicating the Gospel we have, at the very least, to be articulate. Which is different from being loquacious. Most ministers, in the pulpit and out of it, use too many words which distract the ear, much as rococo ornamentation distracts the eye, from the essentials. And few of us have the self-knowledge of the priest who wrote to his mother, 'I think when my birthday comes round you might buy me a muzzle'! Can anything worse be said of a minister than that he likes the sound of his own voice? Although we are word-merchants it is better that we do not love talking; that our talking should be not for its own sake but a tool, or conveyor belt, of truth. 'Let your speech be genuine'—that is what matters.

Theology

An excessively modest friend of mine is for ever declaring that he is not a theologian. I find this irritating for he is a minister and, *ipso facto*, a theologian. It is our business to speak about God, to think about Him, to study His dealings with mankind, and to remove people's doubts and difficulties and bring them to a maturer understanding. All this is theology. You may only have scraped through your classes at college, and be incapable of writing for the journals, but you are none the less a theologian. To say you are not, and even to think you are not, is to betray your congregation. In the pulpit this leads to chitchats on topics of the day or pseudo-psychology on how to relax and obtain peace of mind. This is neither what is wanted nor what you are there to give. They look for some word of the Lord or, better still,

4

from the Lord. You may be a practical man rather than a theorist, and have helpful things to say about the everyday predicaments of your flock: but they must be said *sub specie aeternitatis* otherwise it might just as well be the local bank manager, doctor or social worker who occupies the pulpit and lives in the manse. No; your distinctive subject is theology, 'the things of God,' and you must accept this gladly and, far from abjuring it, keep reminding yourself of it.

A Leader

It was unkindly said, of Franklin D. Roosevelt that he wanted to be the bride at every wedding and the corpse at every funeral. While not going so far, there are some ministers who persuade themselves that there can be no show without Punch. But true leadership is not like that. It should be inconspicuous, unassertive and humble. It belongs to those who know where they are going and share their vision with others without pressing it on them, in the hope and even the confidence that it will catch on. It also means taking the initiative, being decisive and, above all, showing an example.

Some ministers, eager to give a lead, disrupt the congregation's life with a welter of changes, many of them uncalled for and if not overtly then silently resented. At the other extreme are those fearful of rocking the boat. Why not leave well alone, they ask, and why upset the faithful? The true path lies between.

Be prepared, then, to break new ground. But as far as possible take the congregation with you, that change may take place harmoniously rather than disruptively. The breaking and the making have to be linked by the statesmanship of the leader. Simply to ride roughshod over the feelings of one's staunchest members destroys the goodwill on which the success of any innovation depends. For the paramount condition under which changes should be made is that they will promote, corporately and individually, the congregation's true growth.

The best way to establish goodwill is to take the congregation into your confidence. Co-operation is the keynote. The Christian leader, like the biblical shepherd, goes in front; but, like the shepherd, he does not lose contact nor forge ahead on his own. He leads from in front, but not from above. The Welsh have a word for it: *Bid ben bid bont*—'He that would be a leader would be a bridge'. I believe strongly in shared responsibility; and that to be enabled to take some responsibility, however humble, in a church is conducive to spiritual growth.

3 Finding a Parish

The Call

It is only through prayer, self-understanding and the judgement of those who know us best, that we can discern whether any prospective charge may be the one where God is saying, 'Look, I have set before you an open door.'

Ideally a call should come out of the blue and a parish find you. Even so, you must not too readily assume that it is the Lord who is calling. As in everything else, you must test the call 'whether it be of God', and you may find it is not; that a Vacancy Committee somewhere, being as prone as all humans to err, has blundered.

For most probationers, however, the task is one of finding a congenial sphere by their own efforts, and subject to the guidance of God. And the way in which He guides me is not usually by giving me an unreasoned hunch that X, of which I only know the name, is the right parish. But, when I have ascertained all the facts about X, by helping me to sort them out.

This process may continue even when I have reached the stage of preaching before X's Vacancy Committee and meeting with them. Only then may I be able to assess much of the parish's potential, its track record and its leadership resources. When you are interviewed by such a committee you should not leave all the questioning to them. The candidate who asked 'What kind of minister are you looking for?' was on the right tack. You should want to know, for instance, whether the parish has growth potential or is an aged and run-down community; whether the congregation is disheartened and in the red and, if so, are there prospects or portents of recovery? Is there a missionary concern and an ecumenical spirit? What is their spiritual self-assessment? All this is highly relevant.

I would add this word for the discouraged. Should you be continually passed over, and as a last resort accept a far from ideal appointment never forget that opportunity is there, God's people are there, and God Himself is there. There is no situation in which you cannot be used. I think, for instance, of a missionary who, still at the height of his powers, returned from Africa where, in a wide-ranging ministry he had given invaluable leadership, both spiritual and administrative. No home charge showed any interest in him, and eventually he accepted a Home Board appointment to a downgraded congregation which was part of a linked charge; his status being that of Assistant to his young colleague in the major charge. He threw himself into the work to such effect that the congregation was raised again to full status.

It cheers one's heart to hear of such things. But even where there is no recognition one can turn again to Goldsmith's 'Deserted Village' and find solace in his village preacher.

> Remote from towns he ran his godly race,
> Nor ere had changed, nor wish'd to change his place;
> Unskilful he to fawn, or seek for power,
> By doctrines fashioned to the varying hour;
> Far other aims his heart had learned to prize,
> More bent to raise the wretched than to rise...
>
> But in his duty prompt at every call,
> He watched and wept, he prayed and felt, for all.

Today, thank God, such ministers are still to be found—in every kind of parish.

Interlude
'A Bag of Needments' (Chaucer)

You will, of course, build a library. It will gradually reflect your own tastes and needs, and whereas one man's selection will feature pastoralia and homiletics, another's will be dominated by theology and church history. But since to minister widely demands catholicity of mind, a broad range is called for. I would also underline the importance of commentaries; not only William Barclay's with their ready-made illustrative material, but again a wide range, and not all of one school. I myself have close on a dozen, both scholarly and popular, on St John alone; for that is a book from which one constantly preaches.

However small your library, it will contain one or two books which you have found to be of special worth. One such, for me, has been Moorman's *The Path to Glory* (Studies in St. Luke, SPCK) which I refer to again and again. A colleague finds Alan Richardson's *A Theological Word Book of the Bible* invaluable (S.C.M.). Another would go for *The Oxford Dictionary of the Christian Church* (O.U.P.)

As well as the inevitable brief case and a robe case, a sermon case in which your various sheets of paper are placed in order is useful, and if you always use the same size of sermon paper you will come to know how many minutes each page represents.

As pastor and administrator you will be much helped by having filing cabinets and card-indexes; or a combination of folders, large envelopes, notebooks, large and small, desk drawers and small cupboards: and of course a home computer. Whatever the system, you should be able to answer quickly such questions as 'What did I preach on on the last two Christmasses?' 'What were the hymns at the previous quarterly Communion?' 'Is Mrs X in the High Street married, widowed or divorced?' 'What sum was raised for Christian Aid last year?' 'Our missionary partner's address?' 'What did we decide about such-and-such at the committee last October?'

You will have a pocket diary. But should you have a desk one as well? I once did, and it was useful while it lasted. 'I see from the diary that he's got something on that night', my wife would say on the phone. To remember to record everything twice, however, became such a chore that I abandoned it. But have a frequent diary-check with your spouse: each should know the other's commitments.

There are two other pocket-books that the minister requires. The first is a visiting book. Its most useful form is in districts i.e. as a replica of the elders' rollcards. It will have to be replaced after a few years, by which time it will be a mass of emendations but by then it will remind you (assuming you have no card index system) that you called on A in 1982, 1983 and 1988 whereas you have not seen B since 1981.

The other is more ephemeral. It contains the current visiting list—anyone one intends to see this week, with some names carried over from the week before. Not only the housebound and those in hospital, but an Elder here, someone with a problem there, a coming Baptism, a bereavement, a new member, a potential leader, a golden wedding *et al*. And all the memos, ideas and useful information one gleans in the bygoing. I never compiled the parish magazine nor spoke to the local reporter without reference to this notebook, where all the factual data were to be found.

There are also newspapers, radio and television. It is possible to get along without one, or even all, of these. But when you are ministering to Everyman they are vital links. They are also windows on the world, and the world writes the agenda for the Church's mission as for its prayers.

But 'the world is too much with us', and he who would truly serve his fellow-men must also be able to withdraw from them. So the minister needs a Sanctum. The move towards smaller houses, especially when there is a growing family, does not always allow for this. It is not difficult to find a corner, or a table at which to work, but it is harder to get away from people and from noise. In these circumstances it may be possible to make use of the vestry, or even to furnish a garden-hut as a place of retreat. Incidentally, John Baillie, that great scholar, teacher and churchman, devised in a corner of his study a little sanctuary where he prayed.

Among the assets which few ministers can afford to buy is a portable Communion Set. But it can be improvised, and you will certainly need it.

To appear in the pulpit without preaching bands and gown is, to say the least, a mistake. For the established custom is based on two commonsense principles. The first is that the minister is not a layman; his vocation is a unique one; and as he stands before the congregation

9

at the major acts of worship, it should immediately be seen that he is different—for no one else can wear these vestments of his office. The other principle is complementary. Although unique in his office, the minister, as a man or woman, has his own lifestyle, which is partially expressed in his clothes—a woman's dress, a man's choice of shirt or tie, whether a handkerchief protrudes from his pocket or a flower graces his lapel. In the pulpit, however, these personalia distract; and robes are effective in focussing the congregation's attention where it should be focussed—on the service and the preaching rather than on the person of the preacher.

Those who discard the gown believe that they are abandoning what is pretentious and thereby making themselves less conspicuous. Actually they are more conspicuous, especially in the eyes of those who have long been accustomed to the anonymity of pulpit robes.

Part II
WORSHIP AND SACRAMENTS

4 'Let us Worship God'

The primacy of public worship is tacitly acknowledged even by those who seldom attend. Close the doors on a Sunday and there would be an uproar! Whatever else they expect of us this, they believe, is what we are there for. But not many have the imagination to conceive how demanding a task it is.

Adequate preparation—there's the rub. It means willing ourselves to turn from sermon-preparation, which can occupy as much time as we care to give it without ever satisfying us, and thinking about the service. The temptation to skimp the worship is insidious for whereas one can scarcely knock together a sermon in half-an-hour, it is quite possible to do so with a service. A fistful of familiar hymns, two obvious lessons (or three from a lectionary), and the conventional and well-worn phrases of prayer will get you through. But only at the expense of what is vibrant, numinous and enriching; the creative happening that is true worship.

Likewise when the service is unpatterned and disordered is worship impaired. When the prayers are incoherent and rambling, the hymns all of one type, the children's address profuse, the intimations protracted and the sermon 'without form and void', the whole is not only aesthetically but spiritually blemished.

The blend of hymns with lessons, lessons with one another and with the sermon, prayer-themes often related to hymn or sermon and, if it can be arranged, a relevant anthem, should result in a unified, well-proportioned whole. And even though many in the congregation are unaware of any progression, or relationship between the items, it should be there as an undergirding. From praise to penitence, to rejoicing, to dedication and on to outreach is a possible sequence. Or one can begin with *Veni Spiritus* and end with *Laus Deo*.

And there must be a devotional balance. If the service is not to be lop-sided all the great notes should be struck; thanksgiving and penitence, forgiveness and assurance, intercession and dedication, the divine majesty, Christ incarnate, crucified and triumphant, His continuing presence in the Holy Spirit and the call to serve Him. There should be a progression from one to another of these in the mind of the minister as he prepares the worship and in the souls of those who take part.

A service in which the personal note is soft-pedalled is as ill-balanced as one which unduly stresses 'O that will be glory for me'. Where sin abounds in prayer and hymn, with an emphasis on confession and penitence, grace must also abound with an emphasis on the divine love and assurance.

And this all rests in our hands. We are in St Paul's magnificent phrase 'stewards of the mysteries of God'; the mysteries revealed through Word and Sacrament, and through the weekly act of common worship which has always been sacramental or pre-sacramental; and is designed to bring us into communion with Christ whether there is a Celebration or not.

Billy Connolly, the comedian, once remarked: 'In Scotland it's funny, isn't it, you're either a *staunch* Protestant or a *devout* Catholic. I wonder why you're never a *devout* Protestant or a *staunch* Catholic?'

To be devout is to love worship. It is to pray with reverence; to see the church building as the House of God, and to lift up one's heart there, and everywhere, to Him. This surely is what Jesus meant when He said we are to pray 'in spirit'. 'And', He added, 'in truth.'

The language of public prayer
The Lord's Prayer is the touchstone by which all our prayers are tested. And its opening words strike a balance which should be the hallmark of all our worship. God is '*Our* Father' and so the minister does not just pray his own prayers but is the mouthpiece of the congregation. He is 'Our *Father*'and so the language we use is neither precious nor stilted but direct and simple. He is 'Our Father ... *in heaven*' and so, as creatures approach their Creator, and sinners the Holy One, there is reverence and awe.

Public worship should not be over-solemn. Indeed it should be jubilant. 'When do you celebrate public worship?' enquired a visitor from abroad. 'When are the services?' might have been less pedantic but it would not have made me ask myself, Do we *celebrate* worship?

The answer lies in the minister, organist and choir being so attuned to the spirit of worship and to the meaning of everything they do that they will take the congregation with them in the praise and adoration of God.

For us this means more than being 'in the Spirit on the Lord's day'. It requires mental alertness and constant self-criticism. Once you have worked out the details on paper it may seem that all that is left is to announce the hymns, read the Scriptures and the prayers and deliver your sermon. But there is more to it—for we fall easily into bad habits.

In addition to being self-critical we should ask our loved ones what our malpractices are. No one else will dare to tell us that we constantly mispronounce a word; or sniff and pull our ear; whisper or boom; rock or sway; drop our head or roll our eyes; play with our gown or, when musing, speak through our fingers. There are so many things. Some of us, when emphatic, sound petulant and shrill and need to be told to keep on a lower register; others are so lacking in light and shade that we make the most challenging words dull and lifeless. Or we are just wooden.

There is no better beginning to a service than 'Let us worship God', followed not necessarily by the traditional 'Gathering Psalm' but, sometimes, by an invocation of the Holy Spirit or a hymn of adoration or praise.

Before the first prayers it is helpful to have words of invitation either from the scriptures or in well-prepared language of your own. The latter is in Scotland a recent innovation which I find both moving and devotional when it is done well. 'My brothers and sisters in Christ we have come here in His Name in order to ....' or words to that effect. This makes a beautiful lead-in to the prayers of approach and adoration, of thanksgiving, confession and petition which are usually followed by the Lord's Prayer.

What of the general content of the prayers? Acknowledgment of our sins, certainly, but not so much of this as of thanksgiving and intercession; and, always, the communion of saints.

Confession is followed by the plea for forgiveness and for the help of the Holy Spirit. But is this enough? To preach absolution without giving it falls short of our Lord's commission, 'If you forgive any man's sins they are forgiven' (John 20.23). Protestantism in rejecting the claims of Petrine and priestly authority has tended to regard this simply as an assurance that the Church is the forgiving society. It is more than that; a mandate to *apply* forgiveness, not off our own bat but on the authority of the Holy Spirit. The prayer of confession therefore, should be followed not only by 'forgive us' or 'may we be forgiven', but by a Declaration of Pardon, conveyed in one of the authoritative Scriptural sayings.

At a service where the Intercessions reflect concern for the world a stranger will depart without feeling that the act of worship has been myopic and irrelevant; and the congregation through its prayers will grow in concern for the needs of mankind.

No other point in the service can so reflect what is quintessential to the Gospel, 'the passionate participation of the church with the world's pain'. Its drawing to itself 'with thanksgiving and faith, all the joys and sorrows, and achievements, doubts and frustrations of mankind today' (Fourth Assembly of the World Council of Churches, Uppsala, 1968). That, and not twisting God's arm, is what we are doing when we intercede: and this is why the act of intercession should be not a constant pleading and battering at the gates of heaven but the holding before God in expectant faith all that cries out for His concern Who is already there. A pause after each bidding or intercession encourages such 'waiting upon God'.

And always the communion of saints. Not until bereaved myself did I realize how potent a prayer that is. To have our thoughts turned to that whole glorious company in gratitude and love must strike a chord in the hearts of many worshippers. And when a minister omits it, as not infrequently happens, I, for one, feel deprived. Although at other points in the service we have raised our hearts to heaven, only here are we made conscious that it is not only God's dwelling-place but ours; and that already we have a family there.

And what of the Lessons? Shall we take the Authorized Version with its matchless prose; or a modern translation? There is no question but that the Scriptures, if they can be translated into contemporary language which is accurate, graceful and dignified, should be so revised. But it cannot always be said that current versions meet these criteria. They are curates' eggs. And where they are lame and flaccid in language and with a grievous loss of music and rhythms it is obvious that the pendulum has swung too far.

The Blessing

The Blessing, or Benediction, is too often a hotchpotch. It should be sufficient for the minister to raise one or both palms and say 'The grace of the Lord Jesus Christ ...' , or, 'The peace of God ...' or, 'The God of peace ...' , or, 'The blessing of God Almighty ...' But a blessing is not a prayer. A blessing is a blessing. It is the imparting through a simple ritual, and by means of us, His ordained servants, of the favour of God.

When I am in the pew and the officiant fails to say '... be with you all', I feel deprived. Likewise when us is used in a gathering of ministers, for why should a minister not convey God's blessing to his fellows?

At the door

Thus the service ends. But then comes the weekly ritual of shaking hands at the door; followed, in many churches, by coffee in the hall.

For most of my ministry I never went to the door; for I felt that those who wished to see me could do so undisturbed in the vestry; also that at the door people would say thank-you for the sermon—however unworthy it was. I also shrank from what has been called 'the often phoney fellowship of the pally parson's paw and pleasantry in the porch'. I now believe I was wrong. Those with urgent business were few, and at the door would either say 'Can we see you?' or await their chance. And there were always some whom I wanted to see and could talk to briefly 'on the wing'. As for the thank-yous, they were usually sincere; they gave pleasure to those who gave them, and encouragement to myself, and were not numerous enough to be embarrassing.

Whether at the door, or at coffee, one comes to know one's flock better, and they you, and that is gain. And visitors not only come and go, but are made welcome. Someone has referred to this as 'the impossible task of reflecting God's care for each individual'. Yes, it is impossible to do it adequately, but it is still worth doing, even when all you have time for is 'Are you keeping better now?... Good to see you... How's your mother?' One of the difficulties is remembering who people are, or attaching names to faces and you may have to cultivate 'the diplomatic mumble'! You can sometimes drop a brick resembling that of the unfortunate fellow who is reputed to have told Queen Victoria 'I know your face, but I can't recall the name'. But a faulty memory is excused, or unnoticed, if they know that you have a shepherd's heart.

And at coffee, although the prime purpose is that the congregation should meet informally, the opportunity for you to mix around should not be missed, whether or not you have withdrawn to disrobe.

To start with Christmas: one must strike a balance between the Festival of the Incarnation and the Festival of the Child. In some congregations the adults are forgotten and it becomes a children's festival. This is a pity, for St John's Prologue is as central to Christmas as St Luke's narration; and its significance goes far beyond the understanding of children. The incarnation poses crucial and cosmic questions about human destiny and the world's salvation, and proclaims the answers; and this should be declared from the pulpit, as well as being sung in such a carol as 'Hark! the herald angels sing' which encompasses this *mysterium tremendum*.

So I never fail to preach an adult sermon on Christmas Sunday, i.e. the Sunday after Christmas. This is the time when the most mature and thoughtful of our members are present. At the Midnight Service it is a younger and a more mixed congregation to whom the Gospel has to be presented in simpler terms. On Christmas Day it is a family service with only a brief word for the adults, alongside, or incorporating one for the children.

In some churches the Harvest Thanksgiving is turned into a Sunday School service. Understandably so, for the school is there in force and may present the majority of the gifts. And they are certainly to be catered for. But harvest speaks profoundly of death and resurrection, of man's sinfulness in not sharing the divine providence with a hungry world, and of judgment and the last things. This calls for an adult response; as do our Lord's nature-parables and teachings, with their reference to rebirth, growth and fruitfulness. To neglect all this while one gives to the children the simple message of gratitude is to renege on our obligations.

We should also concentrate on that which the occasion celebrates—the miracle of nature, the divine provision, and the renewal of the natural world. It is not the celebration of human creativity, and to display either crafts or the products of industry is misguided. A lump of coal or a glass of water, possibly, but not, as has been known to occur, the intrusion of a typewriter or some other symbol of the congregations's worklife.

If a common failing is to turn the Christmas Sunday service and Harvest Thanksgiving into children's services, the opposite is the case at Easter. Easter Day is now in many churches a Communion Sunday—with either an extra celebration or one of the statutory ones. And the children are forgotten. Parents and children should celebrate the greatest of Festivals together. However Easter is observed I would plead that the children be considered and enabled to share in its triumphant joy.

An occasion which can never be ignored is Remembrance Sunday. It is one which the young minister may face with diffidence and misgivings. The former because he belongs to a post-war generation; the latter because he shrinks from anything approaching jingoism. He may therefore decide to focus on peace and on the pleading in prayer, sermon and praise for the removal of the causes of war.

But this is not enough; especially as there are other peace Sundays. In the next twenty years many in the pews will still have cause to remember those who died; for longer yet the children of the war-dead will be there. So it should remain essentially a service of remembrance; of 'They shall grow not old' and 'We will remember them'. And while the exalting of Queen and Country should be avoided, the service should not be out-of-tune with what takes place at the Cenotaph and in the moving ritual in the Albert Hall. Hymns such as 'Christ is the world's true light' and 'Judge Eternal, throned in splendour' have their place; but not to the exclusion of 'For all the saints' and even the 'ex-directory' 'O valiant hearts' which, minus its reference to 'lesser Calvaries', is the most moving tribute of all.

The temptation, because of the presence of uniformed youth organisations, including their youngest members, to tailor the service for youth should be resisted. It is an act of solemn remembrance and, while there is room for a brief children's address, there are other opportunities, notably at school, for its traditions to be expounded to the young.

The minister's part in public worship has formed the content of this chapter. He has a further concern with worship; the task of teaching people, corporately and as individuals, to pray. Less often now are children taught prayer at their mother's knee, or in family prayers at home; and there is the more need for it to be taught in Sunday School or The Young Church. And this means helping the teachers and directing them to suitable literature and to books of prayers.

An increased proportion of those who come into the Church as adults have escaped the net of Sunday School and, like the disciples, may be asking, Teach us to pray. We can respond in two ways. By preaching on worship; and by not only voicing the congregation's prayers but also directing them. For example, bidding them to pray for this and for that, or calling them to make their confession or their dedication in silence.

I agree with Cardinal Hume that 'harm has been done by a failure to see that prayer is, in the first instance, a waiting upon God in silence' (*Searching for God*, p. 94). In some churches silence is only deeply felt while the Elements are being distributed at Communion. On other occasions, the natural pauses e.g. at the Offering, or when the children leave, are 'covered' by organ music. And if the organ ceased perhaps everyone would talk to his neighbour. For Presbyterians, especially in the northern hemisphere, are activists rather than contemplatives. Should we not, however, teach our people the values of contemplation? 'Be still and know'. It is only through moments or periods of stillness, in church worship, in the house or prayer group, and at home, that our spirituality will grow.

The overall aim in all our worship, expressed in words, music, symbol and silence is this—to make our fellow-worshippers and ourselves aware of God, and of His love towards us through Jesus Christ; and then to lose sight of ourselves and rejoice in Him. And that, surely, is the aim of the Sacraments, without reference to which any discussion on worship is incomplete. They require, however, chapters to themselves, and here I can only endorse what my wife wrote: 'The Sacraments symbolize and convey the free, unconditional grace of God. They have therefore to be quite central to the Church's worship, more so than all our words and striving in praise and prayer and sermon' (Presidential Address to the New College Union, Edinburgh, 1982).

5 Facing the Music

The choice of hymns is best made by the minister, in the context of the service as a whole. The minister who is tone deaf is sorely handicapped. He who is musically illiterate is less so, for this can be overcome. Instead of regretting that he did not learn an instrument in his youth, he should take a crash course in sight-reading. To learn the notes and their values and be able to follow the melodic line, albeit only with one finger, is within anyone's compass. An hour at the keyboard with someone who plays should enable you to use that edition of the hymnary which prints only the basic line: and that will tell you whether it is a known tune or one which promises well. Whether you do this or not, the hymnary on your desk should be a large one; for you need space in which to write beside the hymns the dates on which they were sung. In a year or two a pattern will emerge, and you will know at a glance that while you have sung Hymn A eight times, you have used the equally good Hymn B only once; and that there are sections you have worked too hard and others you have neglected. Also, when someone says, 'Why do we never have So-and-So?' you can verify that we had it last month, and also four months ago!

You should include hymns that are contemporary; for the faith of every age expresses itself in its own terminology and not only in that of the ages that have gone. This does not mean an influx of folk and pop hymns, with artless poetry, ingenuous words, and ephemeral tunes. But it means looking out for the best.

You cannot choose the hymns solely because they have rousing tunes or well-loved words. Their character, style and length should all determine their place in the service. You have to balance one against another; to say, this is quietly devotional and the next should be of challenge or dedication; or, this is demanding, let the next be brief and simple. Or, we have sung objectively of the Church and the world, let us end on the note of personal faith. Or, I have chosen three hymns with similar content and metre, and even from the same century—I must think again.

If you are choosing your hymns with the sermon and lesson in mind, and weaving the service into an integrated whole you should none the less contrive not to make it a one-track affair. Thus, if your theme be Christological there is no need for every hymn to be on the Person of Christ. The opening praise can still take us into the presence of the Almighty, and the final hymn may well—especially if it follows the Intercessions—carry our thoughts out into the world of which Christ is the Redeemer.

A less familiar tune, and strange words, will often win their way if given a chance. And the best chance is by introducing no more than one such in a service, and then neither at the beginning nor the end. To acknowledge that the hymn is unfamiliar will help to defuse any incipient antagonism towards it. You might also add, 'The choir will sing a verse, and then we shall take it from the beginning again'. Nor is this enough: the new hymn has to be sung frequently in the weeks that follow.

In time new favourites will emerge, and for this many will be grateful. Do not, however, ignore the common preference for old hymns; and remember that what may be hackneyed to you will not be so to everyone.

And do not neglect the Psalms. The metrical Psalms and Paraphrases are a priceless part of our Scottish heritage. While there is no obligation to sing them at every service, they should be present more often than they are absent. And I believe our worship would be enriched by the use of some now-neglected psalm-tunes. The 23rd Psalm has become so attached to *Crimond* that *Wiltshire* seldom gets a look-in: we should redress the balance there. And I would resuscitate *Stracathro*, and for Psalm 27 the splendid *Drumclog*. The latter may have been discarded because of its 'twiddly bits'; but to a Scot these are reminiscent of pipe music and far from being incongruous. Similarly I would plead for *Kedron*, long out of fashion. I have seldom been more moved than when it was used for the 30th Paraphrase, at a colleague's funeral. And for *Doversdale* for Psalm 145 and *Desert* (or *Lyngham*) for Psalm 147.

The collaboration of a minister who cares deeply about worship and an organist who is a knowledgeable and sensitive musician is a fruitful one. For the most part, the latter can be given his head, but when the minister foresees a special service, either in connection with the Christian Year or on some other occasion, he should alert the organist. The approach might be, 'Will you mull it over and give me your ideas?', or, 'May I suggest something?'; or, 'Can we have something rather special?'.

To remove an organist, or indeed any church employee, is more difficult than getting rid of guests who have outstayed their welcome. Yet sometimes it has to be done. Dr Garbett, a former Archbishop of York, did not doubt this. He wrote to an uncertain vicar 'Yes, it is a horrid business telling a man that he is past his work, and it doesn't become more easy as one grows older: but clearly you had to change your organist—though he is sure to find a number of foolish people who will support him on the ground that he is a dear old man. We are always in danger of expecting and tolerating a far lower standard of efficiency in the Church than any other profession does' (Charles Smyth, *Cyril Foster Garbett*, Hodder & Stoughton, 1959).

When an organist is dismissed it must be clear that the directive comes from the employing committee; in our case the Kirk Session. Whether it is to be conveyed by letter, or in person by the minister or clerk, should have careful consideration.

And yet, church leadership is, like politics, the art of the possible, and we tolerate standards lower than we would wish; even while taking every opportunity to raise them. Thus when the organist is at a loss for suitable voluntaries and resorts to the Palm Court repertoire, give him for Christmas an anthology of authentic church music!

I have referred to the difficulty of getting rid of an organist but not to the prior and often desperate task of finding one. When advertising brings no suitable candidates what is one to do? There is usually someone in the congregation who can fill in. But the search must go on. Having met with failure the Kirk Session should cast a wide net and also share the problem with the congregation. Meanwhile, the music teacher at the nearest high school is worth consulting. Sixth-formers and school leavers have been a good hunting-ground; though in rural areas the most talented among them soon depart.

My own experience in a rural parish, where we were more than once in straits, is that persistent search (even in advance of actual need) uncovered unexpected resources. Our 'bag' included a retired missionary who had never played in church before, but proved to be excellent; a youth who led a local dance-band (he was so good that when he moved into a nearby town we immediately lost him to a larger church); a retired engineer; a schoolgirl; and the wife of a retired minister.

I suggest that you also tap any musical society in the area, and solicit the help of neighbouring ministers some of whom may have a second string.

At worst, the organ may have to be abandoned. There are pianists and other instrumentalists who, though they will not tackle an organ, might well lead the praise.

Whether or not you take the advice proferred in this chapter, do not undervalue the contribution of music to worship. A dedicated organist and choir performing to the glory of God, and a well-chosen praise list give reality to the summons 'Lift up your hearts'; and to the response 'We lift them up to the Lord'.

6 Preaching: A Joyful Agony

Before we come to the making and delivery of sermons it is necessary to mention the preacher's stance. By stance I do not mean that he should stand steady and not fidget, though that also is true. 'Plant your feet square on the ground,' said James Cagney, 'look 'em in the eye, say what you mean and mean what you say.' Excellent advice, but the question of stance is more subtle than that. Our attitudes are often a giveaway. If we regard the world outside as the enemy, our preaching will inevitably have 'them and us' overtones. But if the world outside consists of others like ourselves, a holy and unholy mixture, with many whose hearts are less selfish than our own, patronizing, denigrating and holier-than-thou attitudes are out.

Those who sit in the pews not only hear what we say (when we remember to speak up) but are aware of our assumptions. 'He treats us all like children' I have heard it said; or 'he thinks we are all theologians'; or 'he was preaching to those who weren't there'. And some of us by being unctuous and ingratiating, or hectoring and censorious, or remote and impersonal, set up barriers.

The prelude to all our preaching has to be an empathy with the congregation and a wide sympathy for all kinds and conditions of men.

Provided that your mind, spirit and imagination are continually active you can approach the task of preaching without the hopeless feeling that there is not a thought in your head. You know that ideas will surface. And in time your facility for gathering sermon-material will increase. Like the journalists, we develop antennae which, as one of them says, 'cast about ceaselessly for stimuli. Whatever they sense is likely some day to be put into words on paper.' And, with that journalist, we need 'other qualities than the ability to put words on paper ... such as curiosity about people, what they do and think, the way things happen' (Mary Stott, *Forgetting's No Excuse*, Faber & Faber, p.102). The ferret's curiosity as well as the squirrel's providence.

But our supreme and never-to-be-forgotten resource is the Bible. It is mandatory for the minister of a Church of the Reformation to familiarize himself with the Word of which he is the servant. To have a mind and heart soaked in Scripture is to possess the equivalent of the widow's cruse which did not run dry. And our main task is to open up the Scriptures; to take their familiar incidents and well-worn words and present them with freshness and power; as one preacher put it, 'to retell with sympathy and vitality the familiar stories so that they come to life and impart life.'

Scotland has a notable tradition of expository preaching. It is epitomised in a remark about that patriarch of the pulpit, Dr Alexander Whyte, of whom it was said that 'his Old Testament and New Testament characters lived and walked the streets of Edinburgh in glory and in shame, and the Edinburgh people discovered that it was themselves he was talking about under ancient Hebrew names.' In a world far removed from that of the Bible such preaching is still relevant. For deeper issues lie beyond the headlines and behind the achievements of science and technology. They are concerned with love and forgiveness, trust and humility, integrity and compassion, man's destiny and his need for God.

Both in their use of the Bible, and in dealing with the contemporary world, many preachers are over-concerned with questions of morality. But this is not the Bible's main business. Behaviour is seen there in relationship to God, from Whom it springs or against Whom it rebels. An obsessive concern for human behaviour and a castigating of immorality is not what preaching should be about. C.S. Lewis shows the way when he says that 'We only learn to behave ourselves in the presence of God, and when the sense of that presence is removed mankind tends to lark about.' So the preacher should concentrate on God rather than on behaviour. Yes, even when he is talking to the children. And when he talks of the Christian life-style he should relate it to its source, as St Paul did when he wrote 'Let your bearing towards one another arise out of your life in Jesus Christ.'

In other words, preaching should be evangelistic not moralistic. But this is not to say that it should be a dogmatic reiteration of 'The Bible says...' 'Jesus says... or, 'Thus says the Lord'. Can a child mature if, when it asks Why must I do this and not do that? it is told, Because I say so? Simply to invoke sanctions from on high is to short-circuit moral maturity. I am averse to any kind of Christian *Diktat*. The emphasis should be on motivation. Behave in this way not because Christ commands it but because in Him you see the rightness and the glory of it; and that you may be like Him and in union with Him. That is the New Testament emphasis. 'The real business of the preacher', as R.L.Stevenson declared, 'is to blow the trumpet for good.' It is to make the love of God known, to make God in Christ visible and audible. And this has to be done not merely in the context of the congregation at worship, but of the world in which our lives are set. Awareness of the contemporary world is the necessary backcloth if our preaching is to be real; but it is not what we are to preach about.

The needs of the congregation will vary considerably. They are not all sinners seeking salvation; many have found it and want to go on from there. Some who have come into the Church with little previous grounding require doctrinal teaching. Some want assurance, while others are too cocksure and have yet to appreciate the uncertainties of our earthly life. For some life runs smoothly, for others it is hell. While many ask, Does existence have a meaning, and is the beyond more than a frail hope?

So a wide variety of sermons is needed, and we must be careful not to pursue any one tack relentlessly. And when we teach doctrine our theological prejudices must be held in check. We must certainly not toe any party line. Nor can our theories of biblical interpretation facilely be identified with the Word of God. It may be so, that worshippers get more from a preacher who is obdurately fundamentalist but fervently sincere than from a lukewarm and wishy-washy liberal. But does this have to be the choice? No form of extremism meets the human condition.

Surely the ideal is the liberal evangelical, the man with a live and questioning mind whose heart yet overflows with the love of God.

There is plenty to preach about. Three hundred years ago an Englishman visiting Scotland remarked that one preacher brought him the majesty of God, another showed him the loveliness of Christ and a third revealed to him his own soul. These are still the quintessential themes. God who has the whole universe in His hands, the Creator in whom alone is our destiny and peace; God at work in history, and today; His goodness, holiness and purpose for mankind. His caring, seeking love in Christ; the wonder of the Incarnation, the splendour of the life and teaching of Jesus, the revelation and saving power of the Cross and Resurrection. The glory and shame of man 'a good thing spoiled', and his rebirth and life in the Spirit.

With all this *embarras de richesses*, to decide on a precise subject may still be difficult. From time to time you can find relief and the congregation some reward by forsaking heterogeneous texts and devising a series. It may be either biblical or doctrinal. A series based on a short book such as Philippians, or a Lenten series on the Beatitudes or The Sermon on the Mount. A Passiontide series on the Seven Words, the great *I am* sayings, or characters of the passion story. A series on parents, teenagers or brothers in the Bible, or on the hills or feasts of the Bible; on Moses, or Peter, or Paul, or the seven churches in The Revelation—the possibilities are endless. But the series should not be overlong—five or six Sundays at the most (even the seven churches need not take seven!).

Preaching becomes anodyne when it is not rooted in reality. Cosy, introverted sermons which never leave Jerusalem to address our condition or to indicate any need for reform in the present social or moral order only bolster the belief that religion is an escape, a 'wings of the dove' affair. The note of judgment is not muted in the Scriptures; nor is the Church's prophetic task. A previous generation was sharply reminded of this by Rheinhold Niebuhr.

There are those at the other extreme, whose down-to-earth sermons become political tracts.

The preacher should open the eyes of his flock in compassion for a hungry and unjust world and in anger against oppression and greed. But his main task is to feed them; and that is better performed by stressing the felicities of heaven and of our life in Christ than by dwelling on the torments of hell and the darker aspects of human nature.

Because it is to the congregation we preach, and not to those who are not there, we must have the congregation in our mind's eye. The congregation—how long-suffering they are! We may prattle on, sometimes in a monotone, delivering sermons of little interest or imagination; predictable stuff with nothing to surprise, bite on or take away. Most of them endure it with amazing loyalty and scarcely a murmur, though this presumably is why others stay away.

The congregation will consist largely of long-standing members who have again and again committed themselves to Christ and to His way of life. The conventional churchgoing of unbelievers is a thing of the past. If we assume the role of a sheepdog chivvying at their heels, and for ever exhorting and challenging them, rather than that of a shepherd, we will exasperate them, as Admiral Collingwood was exasperated when he burst out, 'I wish Nelson would stop signalling: we all know what to do.'

Admittedly there are some who only turn up at the quarterly Communion (or, in England, at the festivals), less to worship than to maintain their standing, or in case they should one day require the minister's help. But these laggards may well be believers who are too undisciplined to forgo the preoccupations of other Sundays. To take advantage of them at Communion or on Christmas Eve by belabouring them for their lukewarmness is tactless in the extreme. It will either scare them away or nourish their aversion to regular churchgoing.

Similarly, it is futile to preach at, or try to set right, some individual or faction. Scolding misfires.

On controversial topics

On political credos and topics of great public controversy such as disarmament, abortion and capital punishment, and on the questions raised about divorce and industrial and race relations, we may have strong convictions. It is one thing to share them but another to claim that they are the only possible positions for a Christian to take. I find it astonishing, as well as disconcerting, when ministers lay down the law on complex questions. Such dogmatism is foolish. Our parishioners, though they differ from one another, find little difficulty in worshipping and serving their church together. But when they differ from us and we take advantage of the pulpit, or of our positions, to advocate views which are either strongly radical or doggedly conservative, those who have to suffer in silence are justifiably resentful. This is not to say that we should hide our convictions; in discussion they are bound to be revealed; and there are times when on some big public issue we are impelled to speak out, and many will be grateful when we do.

Acknowledging Doubt

We should also realize that, even in a believing congregation, belief will be tempered with doubt. 'Preach your certainties, not your doubts' say most of the textbooks; but in a questing age this is dubious advice. The integrity that admits doubt is more likely to win respect and to open thoughtful minds to the truth than is glib certitude.

For sure, the trumpet note must sound. The positive must be dominant. There must be good news. But to conceal real difficulties, for instance concerning miracles or 'hard' sayings, is less than candid; and to declare more than one believes, dishonest. Whereas to enter into, and maybe to share, some of the uncertainties which are common to all but the simple-minded, and to say so frankly, is the way to a deeper faith.

Although many want to know that we understand their doubts, and are allergic to easy answers, they also need assurance. And we too must speak 'with authority and not as the scribes.' The rejection of dogmatism and authoritarianism is not the repudiation of authority. People will listen, as they did in Jesus' day to the authority of one who knows what he is talking about. Each parish requires what Carlyle said Ecclefechan needed, 'someone who will speak of God not merely from hearsay'. One who does not shout, quibble or beat about the bush, but is quietly convincing. Who is not forever pussyfooting round the truth with 'It may be...', and 'I suppose...', and 'It seems to me...'; but who can say, 'I assure you', and 'I tell you this', and 'Believe me'. (These last three are modern translations of 'Verily, verily I say unto you'.)

The classic expression of the preacher's motivation is, after all, that given by St John in the first five verses of his first epistle '...What we have seen and heard we declare to you...'

The Practicalities

How does one set about the task and deliver the goods? What happens when you sit at your desk and take up your pen?

But first, for how long should you shut yourself away in the study? A busy parish minister can feel guilty because he gives so little time to sermons—or because he gives so much.

When someone is endowed with a special gift he should spend a great deal of time on it. Those who are born preachers, with this special gift from God, are justified in the priority they give to it. The world has need of them, and they should not dissipate their energies by taking on much else beyond their pastoral responsibilities. If we are not in that category (and most of us are not) we should give sermon preparation a less exclusive priority but a high one nevertheless. As many mornings as possible when the mind is fresh; though not as many as our forefathers, undistracted by school and other chaplaincies, were able to give. Most of our sermons are written under pressure.

To take a text, and to return to it again and again, and not depart from it at the end is one way in which to produce a disciplined sermon. It also gives to the hearers something to which they can link your message and by which they may remember it. Without it you will often be casting about for a theme.

Only rarely will someone give you a peg by saying, 'I've never heard a sermon on...' or 'I always feel sorry for...' (Martha, or Pilate, or the Elder Brother). And when none of the texts in your notebooks takes fire you have to find one—so make it one of the great ones on which you know you must preach some day. It will be more than a peg; it will give you its own insights which are the very thoughts of God.

The sermon may have to be appropriate to a particular Sunday. If it is a Sunday integral to the Christian Year or earmarked for a special purpose there is little problem. But it is inadvisable to preach every year on, say, the Presentation in the Temple, or the Conversion of St. Paul, or on St. Andrew. All Saints, on the other hand, need never be ignored, offering as it does a variety of emphases and of texts. John the Baptist I find awkward, in that he is both an Advent figure and one associated with the third Sunday after Christmas and also with Lent. Common sense tells me not to overdo him, and a dozen sermons in as many years on the man and his message would seem a maximum. Of all the other Sundays assigned to New Testament characters and events there are none which I would wholly abandon but few which I would observe annually.

Slow boil or pressure cooker?
Before you clear your cluttered desk for action there is one more question to be answered. When do you get down to it? At the beginning of the week, or near its end? Slowly to the boil, or the pressure cooker? As one whose thoughts have always simmered slowly my instinct is to scorn the latter; but I must not, for it has been successfully used, both from choice and of necessity. Its Scottish archpriest, some say, was the late Dr Harry Whitley of St. Giles', a controversial figure but no mean preacher. He would tell his assistants that if they wanted to preach 'with fire in the belly' that is how they should set about it. Sweat it out on Saturday night and, if need be, into the early hours of Sunday, then deliver it red-hot. But for most of us more careful preparation is needed: much agonizing, brooding and thinking.

It does not much matter what the shape of a sermon is, but a shape it must have. Asked whether his films had a beginning, a middle and an end, a French director replied, 'Yes, but not necessarily in that order.' The story of Zacchaeus can illustrate well what he meant. It has a clear beginning—Zacchaeus in the tree; a middle—the encounter with Jesus; and an end —Zacchaeus reborn. But the preacher need not follow that sequence. He can begin at the end and ask how this startling conversion came about; or in the middle with Jesus picking out Zacchaeus from the crowd, and work backwards and forwards from there. Not only do these less obvious approaches enable you, and others, to see the story afresh; but they also mean that you do not have to forbear from preaching on Zacchaeus again because you 'did' him only two years ago.

Manifestly the beginning and the ending merit especial attention. Whoever said 'Grab 'em at the beginning and zip it up at the end' said it all. Yet one still hears too many sermons which are either slow in getting up steam or chunter to a halt like a train with faulty brakes.

When I write a sermon and find it to be too long the fault usually lies in the introduction. I plunge in at page three, and it comes right!

The message is clear: don't rabbit around, but get to the point. And in the middle keep up the momentum. Although occasionally you should slacken pace, perhaps be use of anecdote or illustration, you must beware of rambling. As for the ending, let it be neither a swollen peroration nor an abrupt pulling of the plug, but a definite conclusion. And this may take a variety of forms; a summing up or a challenge, a recapitulation of the text, a phrase or a crystalline quotation to re-member, or sometimes a heartfelt arrow prayer.

Delivery

Some say that preaching, like nostalgia, is not what it used to be. Perhaps they are only being nostalgic themselves, and regretful that the polished literary efforts, studded with quotations from Browning, have given way to a more conversational style. But students fresh from college still produce sermons in the style of students' essays, and the voice of the religious cliché, like that of the turtle, is heard year by year in the land!

Young people inevitably speak in jargon; especially on religious matters. They have not yet found their own voice and have to use ready-made terms. When I hear a preacher say 'But let's face it,' or 'at this point in time,' or 'a viable situation,' or 'a nonsense' my heart sinks. Are his thoughts so second-hand and has he a commonplace mind? Or is he just slipshod?

We need not, however, avoid colloquialisms, the use of which can be extraordinarily effective. Recounting the conversation of Jesus with the woman by the well, a preacher said, 'Jesus told her to bring her husband. 'I haven't got a husband' she said. 'You can say *that* again,' said Jesus, 'you've had five of them!' —and the dialogue came to life. Similarly, to say that the boy Jesus at Jerusalem 'led his parents a bit of a dance' expresses what they might well have said. And if Pilate 'washed his hands of Jesus', his action was in fact the origin of the phrase. Nor in speaking lucidly and directly need we preach without felicity. The arresting phrase, the apt simile, the avoidance of hackneyed quotations and platitudes and the accurate use of well-chosen words will enforce our message.

What makes a poet is initially that person's love of poetry fostered, even in a genius such as Burns, by reading other poets. What makes a preacher is a love of preaching fostered by studying other preachers. And this is why most of us read voraciously about our craft; hoping, perhaps, to find the elusive alchemy that will turn our leaden efforts into sparkling gold. But resist the temptation to reproduce a ready-made sermon, which is wanting in that subtle element of personal thought which captures the mind and heart. Deliver your own message. Cf. Julian Barnes's advice that writers 'be issued with a sampler in coloured wools to hang over the fireplace. It reads: Knit your own stuff' (*Flaubert's Parrot*, London: Cape, 1984, p. 99).

To find your own voice and style takes many years. But in the meantime? In the meantime you can, at the very least, avoid all semblance of a pulpit manner. To thine own self be true is a platitude, but how crucial for the preacher! As Jane Austen determined to remain Jane Austen, and not to adopt any other persona. To the kind suggestion that she should write on another sort of subject in another manner she wisely replied: 'I am fully sensible that an historical romance, founded on the House of Saxe Cobourg, might be much more to the purpose than such pictures of domestic life in country villages as I deal in. But I could no more write a romance than an epic poem... No, I must keep to my own style and go on in my own way; and though I may never succeed again in that, I am convinced that I should totally fail in any other' (Letter, 1 April 1816). Scott said that he himself could do 'the Big Bow-Wow strain,' but knew he was denied 'the exquisite touch' of Jane Austen. An artist even while he is finding himself must, paradoxically, be himself.

However vivid, telling and, above all, revealing our sermons are it remains true that what we say without love—though we speak with the tongues of men and of angels—is of no effect. What we are speaks louder than what we say and he who is unskilled with words and bungles his sermons, but who has this grace of love towards God and men, may feed the flock better than his more talented brother.

Sunday comes and you ascend the pulpit. But how? In high spirits and brim-full of confidence, or with trepidation and a silent 'Help me, O God'? To have the former without the latter is to court spiritual disaster; but to feel the frisson of fear, without also knowing the freedom and joy of the Gospel, is also to dishonour one's trust. The two should co-mingle.

Audibility

The inaudible sermon is a dead loss. I am saddened by the many occasions when, at the door of a strange church, someone has told me 'I heard every word you said'; implying that they could not hear their own minister. I happen to be blessed with good lungs but there is little excuse for most mumblers. With many it is just a bad habit, or they lack the imagination to see that the decibels of the drawingroom will not reach the back pew. To speak out is a golden rule, and one should be aware of the requirements and the 'dead' spots of one's own church building. We should speak emphatically and sometimes with passion. Even when you are reading closely you should look at the congregation.

If there is no public address system and you are cursed with feeble vocal chords, and cannot turn up the volume, what then? Well, it is not only a matter of decibels. Alec Robertson, the musicologist was once, as a secular priest, on the staff of Westminster Cathedral, and had to preach from the big nave pulpit. 'I soon discovered,' he wrote, 'that the secret of being heard in that vast space—there were no microphones in use then—lay in the utmost clarity of enunciation and as wide a range of inflection as possible, not in the use of a great volume of tone. There were priests who shouted their way through their sermons and in consequence remained inaudible at the back of the church' (*More than Music*, Collins, 1961, p. 170).

To accept your limitation *and to do nothing about it*—that is the real sin. The thousands of sermons lost in the waste-bin of our inaudibility are not only squandered—like a cook furnishing a fine meal only to throw it away uneaten—they are a discourtesy to our hearers; and a grieving of the Holy Spirit Who collaborates in the making of every true sermon.

Emotion

We should preach not only clearly but with feeling. Most of us when we preach a dry sermon do so not because we are dry-as-dust scholars dwelling on minutiae of interpretation, but because we lack intensity and conviction, emotion and rapture, drama and passion. It may be the lack of drama in our pulpits—as in our worship—that causes many young people to write off the Church as spineless and lukewarm.

There is no place for exhibitionism in the pulpit; but there are moments when what we are saying about the mercy of God, the grace and love of Jesus, and the Christlike spirit and selfless deeds of His followers will move us deeply. Should we not show it? Dr James Black, to many the greatest preacher of his day, was emotional, but there was no affectation, and his emotions were under control. His role was to ignite. The drama and passion of his preaching broke through the native reticence of a Scottish congregation and brought many of my generation to commitment to Jesus Christ. His book *The Mystery of Preaching* is still rewarding. But what I learned most from him is not in a book. It is that we should preach always from a full heart and sometimes, whether the congregation can see them or not, with tears in our eyes.

Sharing the pulpit

Others will occupy your pulpit when you are on holiday. But should you relinquish it at other times? For a number of reasons some ministers never absent themselves; because of the inconvenience of arranging an exchange, or because they do not feel at home in a strange church, or through an exaggerated sense of obligation, or even of insecurity. But if our obligation is to feed the flock we may well fulfil it best by arranging for them an occasional change of diet. It is good for a congregation to hear a fresh voice; especially for one with a young minister to hear an older one and *vice versa*; as well as being for your own refreshment. Similarly, some ministers will not invite an unlicensed preacher into their pulpit. They consider preaching to be so important that those who are trained for it must keep it in their own hands. But this is too limited a view.

In scriptural exegesis and doctrinal exposition the untrained layman is at a disadvantage; and he cannot adequately occupy the same pulpit for long periods. But we dare not stand with the Jewish Sanhedrin who noted that Peter and John were untrained laymen and ordered them to refrain from preaching (Acts 4.13 ff.). The Methodists are right. The layman's witness can be more effective, just because he is a layman, than our own; and we should seize opportunities to let him be heard.

The efficacy of the ephemeral

When all has been said on preaching, the doubt may still assail us: is it worth the candle—and the sweat? For, after all, sermons are ephemeral and by Wednesday most church members will have forgotten what we said.

Even while we write them we may grow despondent. For inspiration flags and the pen becomes 'as the oars to a galley slave'. Or, drained after preaching, we groan at having to begin the whole process again, and yet again.

Yes, sermons are ephemeral. But that does not invalidate their worth. But to allay all doubt one has only to recall a morning in Galilee when Jesus preached from Simon Peter's boat. We do not know what He said, and Peter and his friends may soon have forgotten the gist of it, but the effect was plain to see. Dispirited fishermen again set sail and cast their nets. It can happen still. The sermon becomes the vehicle of His word which ignites and empowers. It is as our forefathers used to say, 'a converting ordinance', a tool, a lever, a means of grace. This thought should dispel all doubt. It should also prevent us from soporific utterance, and make the labour of sermon-preparation a creative and joyful agony.

7 Baptizing Babies

Discriminating

Most Churches repudiate indiscriminate baptism. But how to discriminate is one of the trickiest of questions.

One thing is certain; that when we hear of a birth we should not go round peddling Baptism as if it were as available as maternity benefits on the National Health Service. It is not for us to make the decision for any parents that they should have their child baptized. It must be their desire and their decision, and then we shall give an answer. Whether that answer be yes, no, or, less dismissively, not yet, it must be a truly Christian one. Warm and positive where there is no dubiety; tender and caring where there is. When the answer is no, it should be either, 'This is not the church you should have him baptized in, and we will help you to make contact elsewhere'; or, 'I still hope to do it, but I think you should go home, now that you know more about it, and see if this is what you really want and if you can honestly take the vows.'

When we give our verdict we are bound in the course of a long ministry to make mistakes. And I must say that I would rather err by saying yes than no; and feel unhappy at refusing the sacrament to any who ask for it. For whenever we say no, and especially when the parents feel that not only they but their baby has been rejected—and by those who stand for Him who said 'Suffer the little children... and forbid them not'—alienation from the Church and bitterness towards religion may set in.

Our forefathers said that Baptism was 'for the seed of the faithful'. But the crunch question is, who are they? Those faithful to the Church? Or having faith in Jesus Christ, a faith which ought to, but does not invariably, lead to church membership? All church members are not faithful, but must all the faithful be church members? Did not our Lord say of an outsider, 'I have not found such faith even in Israel'? How do we differentiate and draw the line?

I myself would draw it widely. I would not reject the young mother who confessed that she had come to please her Gran without asking, 'But do you agree with your Gran?' Nor turn away those seeking a magic charm without disabusing them of their superstition and looking behind it for any evidence of faith or new understanding.

It is frequently suggested that we should offer those from whom, for one reason or another, we would withhold the sacrament a non-sacramental service of Blessing. The proposal is a compassionate one. Instead of sending the parents away with an apparent snub because they have not measured up to the Church's standards, would this not be something positive? We could at any rate assure them of the Saviour's love for children, and tell them that as He blessed those brought to Him in Galilee, He will bless their children still. And we could devise a simple service in which thanks was said for their coming, and their homes were prayed for and the parents' marriage vows renewed.

But I am not so sure. For such a service might well be regarded as a surrogate baptism, an alternative rite. When a mother wants her child baptized and the mother next door takes no similar action, that is understood, and is normal. If, however, they should both go to the minister and one be granted Baptism but the other something which resembles it, the second parent might well assume, 'Well that's it. My baby has been "done". He has had all that is given to a non-church family, and needs nothing more.'

Time and Place

With regard to date, one has to be flexible. Someone will tell you that their sister, who is to carry the baby, is nursing a hundred miles away, and can only be present on a certain weekend; or that the grandparents hope to come, but run a business and can only make it at the Whitsun holidays; or that the father, in the Navy, has only a brief shore leave. As far as possible I try to meet such circumstances, and if the congregation find themselves with baptisms on successive Sundays or on a Communion Sunday, I explain why.

The place, of course, is the church; though there are still a few who demur at this. If so, you take the chance to do a little teaching. You explain that it is a sacrament which Our Lord gave not to families but to the Church. 'The child belongs to your family; now he is to be welcomed into his second home, the family of the Church. And the congregation's part is to welcome him into that family. In Scotland the congregation are also the godparents. They will be asked to receive your child, and to help in his upbringing. I shall be telling you later how we do this—through Cradle Roll and Sunday School and the

36

Church's concern for your home, and its prayers. All of which makes the Church the fitting place.'

If they still demur, for reasons such as the father's unavailability, the shyness of a single parent, or reluctance to present older children on a public occasion, I tell them that nevertheless the House of God is the fitting place, and that if it has to be on a weekday, or after the Sunday service, the congregation will be represented by an elder, a teacher, and/or other appropriate persons.

There are, of course, exceptions, such as cases of extended illness. So, as in all activities, occasions arise when you have to bend the rules. When Jesus said 'The Sabbath was made for man, not man for the Sabbath', He meant just this—that a rigidity which admits no exception is wrong.

The Interview

In the interview I would begin by talking about the family. I then introduce them to the service and the vows, and explain what it is all about, being careful to relate to their understanding. Some need it in words of one syllable; others, intelligent and articulate, may want to know what we mean by grace, or why we invoke the Trinity. Incidentally, if any have doubts or difficulties about the Trinity, or say that 'Three-in-One and One-in-Three' is mumbo jumbo to them, I find George MacLeod's definition an excellent lead-in. The Trinity, he said, is 'God here, there and everywhere.' Here, the Holy Spirit: there, the historical Jesus: everywhere, the Creator of all things and Father of us all.

Basically there are two vows, although the Book of Common Order presents them as three questions. My own practice is to frame them as just two questions, the first calling for a profession of faith, the second for a promise.

1) *Do you confess your faith in God as your heavenly Father, in Jesus Christ as your Saviour and Lord, and in the Holy Spirit as your Helper?*

2) is a promise which includes Christian nurture and example, and the completion of Baptism in communicant membership. Nowhere have I found this expressed more clearly and directly than in the Order of the Church of South India, whose phrases I have collated into a single question. *Do you Promise by God's help to provide a Christian home for this child; to bring him up in the ways of the Church of God; so to order your own lives that you do not cause this little one to stumble;*

and to encourage him later to be received into the full fellowship of the Church?'

'Let's take that bit by bit,' I would say at the interview. 'Surely these are the things you want to do. *To provide a Christian home*—but what does that mean? Not just a home with pious God-talk, though He should be talked about, but one full of loving care, of companionship, of patience and forgiveness and unselfishness, and everything that is Christlike. And where Christ is held in honour.' '*In the ways of the Church of God*—and most parents know that their children need the Church, even when they are not so sure that *they* do.' '*To order your own lives*—because example is all-important.' '*To encourage him later*—because Baptism looks forward to the day when they will profess their own faith. The vows you now make, you hope they will make.' (But I never say, 'The vows you make *on their behalf.*' It is not *on their behalf*; these are the parents' own vows.)

I then run through the service, not omitting the practical details. 'At this point the church officer brings you in, and at this he takes you out. Whoever is carrying the baby gives him to the father, who gives him to me (I'll tell you when). And get his head in your right arm, if you can, so that I will have him in my left and be able to sprinkle with my right hand; and I'll give him back to his mother, so that you will both be in the picture, as it were. And, by the way, hymnbooks will be open on the chairs and I'll show you the place in the first hymn. And don't forget to bring the birth lines, and I'll sign on them that he has been baptized.' (Alternatively, the procedure can be set out in a leaflet.)

Occasionally a mother will tell you that the father is not coming. Sometimes you have to accept this and go ahead. But often you can persuade him that it is just as much his affair, and that if he cannot honestly take the vows he can at least stand with his family while his wife takes them. Once when a father had come, on my insistence, to the interview, I thought he had got the message. But on the day of the Baptism, which for some reason was a weeknight, the mother appeared alone. 'Where's the father?' I asked. 'Oh he's outside holding the dog.' We tied up the dog, and got him in!

The Service
The Book of Common Order says 'It is assumed that Holy Baptism normally follows the preaching of the Word'—by which is meant that

it follows the Sermon. This is traditional but not sacrosanct and many prefer to have it at the beginning of the service.

You may have no choice in the matter. But where there is a choice I would opt for the beginning.

First, because I believe the Word should have a direct bearing on the sacrament, and should be a means of grace to all present and especially to the parents. Now while the main sermon can be related to the Baptism it cannot always be so, especially if you are having baptisms every month; or it can only be so by contrivance: and if it happens, as it often does, that the sermon is your only Easter, or Whitsunday, or All Saints Day utterance, it is not only awkward, but a pity if you have to gear it towards the Baptism when its whole thrust should be towards the Festival.

Moreover it is unlikely that the parents will be present during the sermon. You may still give a brief Word at a post-sermon sacrament, but coming after the fuller sermon it will detract from it, and psychologically is in the wrong place. A baptismal talk at the beginning, however, stands by itself and supplies the need of parents and congregation alike.

Secondly, in most churches the children are present, then go out to Sunday School. To bring them in again for a later Baptism disrupts their syllabus for which there is always too little time.

Thirdly, with the Baptism early I can greet the family (who often know no one else) and put them at their ease. I also used to introduce them to the Elders who gave them a warm welcome. That they were there when I prayed with the Elders while the Beadle took the Bible in—for such was the practice—enhanced their impression of the Church.

The Order of Service should be simple. First a short prayer of invocation, for there is no room for such in the sacrament. Then praise which might, or might not, be a baptismal hymn. If not, I nevertheless would often find in it the text for the talk. It might be only a phrase like 'God of our fathers! be the God of their succeeding race.' Or a Psalm like the 8th with its question, 'What is man that Thou art mindful of him?' Or a whole hymn: 'The Church's one foundation' and 'Glorious things of thee are spoken' touch throughout on the meaning of Baptism.

The family should be ushered in at the very start of this hymn, so that they can participate; likewise they should stay till the last couplet of the next hymn, and if that means a hiatus before the Lessons, that is all to the good. The pause will mark a change of key.

Before the talk I announce the name and address of the child. For those who are welcoming him into their midst should not only hear his Christian name but be able to identify him. I then say what I have to say, which may have to be curtailed even drastically if the baby sets up a cacophony. The talks are related to the occasions. These vary both Sunday by Sunday, and parent by parent. A baptism at Harvest Thanksgiving evokes thoughts of beginnings and of growth; on Palm Sunday, of the response of children to Jesus; in Christian Aid Week, of the dignity and value of human life; and every Sunday has its special message.

But one should also ask if the message is geared to that particular family. For some it is the first baptism, for others the third or fourth; some are more, others less attached to the congregation; some come from a broken home, or one with mixed faiths. A family is briefly home from abroad, another about to emigrate. We should be sensitive to such things.

After the talk, the sacrament. I take the baby in my arms to baptize him; and often explain that this symbolizes the parents saying 'He belongs not only to us but to God', so they give him to the Church; but the Church gives him back as if to say, 'Yes, but you are the trustees.' I also, as I sprinkle the water, do so in the sign of the Cross, a practice more Anglican than Presbyterian, but no less acceptable for that. The words of the Anglican Prayer Book are explicit: 'We receive this child into the congregation of Christ's flock, and do sign him with the sign of the Cross, in token that hereafter he shall not be ashamed to confess the faith of Christ crucified...'

To the parents, after 'enable you faithfully to keep these promises,' I would say, 'Let your light so shine before men...'; words whose inspiration some of us have felt in the Toc H Ceremony of Light. And after the declaration that the child is now received I would add the wonderful words: 'Jesus said, Whoever receives one of these little ones in my name receives me.'

The Follow Up

You yourself, if you have many baptisms, may not be able to follow them up, except for looking in at the christening party, if invited. But the congregation should. I was always able to tell the parents that the Cradle Roll secretary would call; or she might already have done so.

Also that she would put the baby's name on the Cradle Roll and send a card on his first two birthdays, and on his third an invitation to the Beginners Department. But very soon, I would add, you will be invited to bring him to a cradle roll service, when there will be a great parking of prams and the Primary children will sing and present posies.

All these, and possibly a creche during services and a church-run playgroup, are ways in which congregations carry out their baptismal promises. Their youth programmes and the elders' care for the families in their districts are also the follow-up.

Adult Baptism

In a congregation where adult baptisms rarely occur, it will be a considerable ordeal for a diffident person to be publicly baptized. Therefore, though I would encourage an adult to be baptized at the confirmation service, pointing out the witness they would be making, I would not insist on it; and I have baptized some on weeknights. One whom I remember was a lady well into her eighties who said it troubled her that she had never been baptized and would I do it before she died? Since she knew all about Baptism and was already, by some circumvention, a church member, I called in the Session Clerk and baptized her there and then in the vestry.

What should you do if someone, an elder say, came to you and said that they either had been or wished to be re-baptized? If he said he had been re-baptized I would not reply 'You have broken the laws of the Church'. I would ask Why? And he would tell me of some charismatic experience through which he had met the living Christ and become 'a born-again Christian'. 'That's wonderful', I would say, 'and I understand how you want to mark it, and to respond. But you have not understood the meaning of your first baptism; its validity, and sufficiency and rightness.'

Where the second baptism is not a *fait accompli*, I would say, 'I know you want to thank God and to give yourself to Him in a special way. Can I give thanks with you now and then we'll talk about it.' And I would speak of the sufficiency of infant baptism and suggest that the kind of response he now wants to make is mistaken but that there are other ways. If the normal Communion service does not meet his need, why not a special Communion of intent where only a few would gather and a personal prayer or act of commitment be inserted? Or if he sees adult baptism as an act of witness, would he be willing instead to make

41

his witness before the whole congregation or some part of it by telling them briefly what has happened to him?

The Church's approach should be tender and positive to the individual, however firmly it stands by its baptismal standards. At the same time I wonder whether the desire for a second baptism does not point to the Church's need for something else. A way of marking the Damascus road experience which is undergone, perhaps increasingly in our time, by church members. Something vivid, and even dramatic. It might correspond to the penitent stool of the Salvation Army or the covenant service of Methodism. Easter, with its symbolism of death and resurrection, or Pentecost would seem suitable annual occasions for such a non-sacramental spiritual baptism.

There is also the question of baptizing neither infants nor adults but young children. In baptizing a girl of twelve, I asked her to express her own faith and make her own promise; but also asked her parents to reaffirm their vows. From Sunday School age children can understand Baptism and I would talk with them and not only with their parents beforehand. Just as we are now thinking of talking with young children about Communion and preparing them for it.

This first of Sacraments is both a supreme treasure of the Church and the best of all its evangelical opportunities. The first because it encapsulates so tenderly the Gospel of the free grace and individual love of God; the second, because it is an opportunity to lead parents towards Christ and to give them the sustaining fellowship of His Church.

8 Preparing Communicants

Not every minister sees the Communicants' Class as a golden opportunity. I have known some who have given their confirmands only the briefest of briefings in the highly dubious belief that, except for some elucidation on Holy Communion, they knew it all and had no need for more. This is a strange assumption, especially nowadays when few class members will have had the extensive training of Sunday School and Bible Class. Many will have been in neither, or the Sunday School will only have held them to the age of eight or ten. As for their secondary school, the instruction they received there (before religion became an 'O' Level subject) was probably minimal, and possibly consisted of a scamper through the world religions.

Even the middle aged are often ill-versed in the faith, and among otherwise mature people there are many with naive notions and unexpected gaps in knowledge.

Here then is a golden opportunity for Christian education: '...a happy work, such as will do more for the welfare of the Church than many that the world doth make a greater stir about' (Richard Baxter on 'the private instructing of the flock', *The Reformed Pastor*, 1655). The field is clear for you to teach the Faith and to share your enthusiasm for and vision of the Church. To muff that opportunity is, by implication, to convey a defective and trivialized image of the Church, and even of Christianity as things of low esteem. 'Easy come, easy go' is an adage too often verified in the experience of the Church and those who join it.

'A lifelong commitment to the Church,' I would tell the candidates, 'is a decision not to be taken lightly. It could even be that, after several weeks in the class and knowing more fully what it is all about, you will find you are not ready for it. In that case, you don't have to be confirmed; but I hope you will have enjoyed the class and will come back again. I hope even more that you will find that the time is now; but we shall see.'

You may well have a very mixed bunch. Some will be serious and expectant, looking for teaching and guidance, for Christian assurance and an inspiring vision of the Kingdom. For some the decision to come has not been easy, while others are not certain that they should be there. There are those with such a love for Christ and His Church that they want to 'plight their troth', and feel that they are approaching a summit. And there may well be an older couple who, for their own and their children's sakes, are finally taking the plunge.

Mutual introductions having been made, and the ice broken with some conversation, possibly about their interests and occupations, I would record their names. Then 'Before we get down to it' I would say, 'I think we should start with a prayer.'

I would then proceed to outline the ground to be covered. 'Today I'm going to talk about that phrase "joining the Church" and what it means. If you were baptized, haven't you already joined? How is this related to your baptism? (If any of you haven't been baptized, let me know.) And this Church you are joining or being received into—is it just the local church, or the Church of Scotland, or the whole world-wide Church to which all denominations belong? Or all three?'

'Then I shall go on to tell you what happens at the Confirmation Service. What vows will you be asked to take? And what is it that is being "confirmed"? Your parents' promises at your baptism? Or are you confirming your own faith? Or is God confirming His promise to you?'

'After that we'll have a look at the history of the Church: a bird's-eye view. What do you know, for instance, about Luther and Calvin, and John Wesley? What happened at the Reformation? And what about our own Church—why is it Presbyterian and what does that mean? Who were St. Columba and John Knox and what did they have to do with it? And what of the Church today, our own and other denominations?'

'We'll go on to ask, What does the Church believe? A historic statement of Christian belief is the Apostles' Creed which we will study. (It's in the Hymnbook.) There are strange things in it like "He descended into hell" and "the resurrection of the body". What on earth do they mean? We'll discuss that. We will have to spend three or four weeks on the Creed.'

'Then we can have only a brief look at the Bible. And there's prayer, which is a problem to many people. And, since this is the congregation you are joining you had better know its story and how it is run.'

'Then there are the services—let's look at them and see what goes on and what we do when we worship.'

'And the question we can't avoid, of who pays for it all. I'll ask the Treasurer to come along and explain the finances; and he'll tell you about those envelopes you see people putting in the plate.'

'Towards the end as we come near your first Communion I'll go through the Communion Service with you, and we'll ask what it means, the Bread, the Wine, the Table and how Christ is present in it all.'

Another essential topic is the loyalty demanded in the confirmation vows. Can one make lifelong promises without perjury? How do I know I will be as faithful in ten years time? These questions, I point out, might also be raised regarding the marriage vows. And the answer is the same. First, what you promise must be your sincere intent. Second, if you find yourself 'ratting' on your vows you can always renew them. And third, there is in Christianity the promise of forgiveness and the Holy Spirit, so that whenever we fail, as we will, we can begin—or be begun—again.

That, in brief, is the programme. It is obvious that it can take anything from eight weeks to six months or a year to cover it. My own practice was to have two intensive eight-week classes per year. Once, however, I was asked by the Kirk Session to extend them. They had been worried by the fact that as the class went on, its members were conspicuously absent from the services. 'If they can't come now they won't come later—they'll appear at one Communion and we won't see them again.' So we postponed the Confirmation for another three months and put them on probation. When I explained this to the Class they took it well, and agreed to continue meeting, though not every week. And the result was a greater loyalty.

I sometimes wonder whether we do not admit candidates too easily, in another way; by omitting to lay upon them any particular demand, such as memorizing certain passages, or studying certain books of the Bible. Ninety years ago Dr Macgregor of St. Cuthbert's, Edinburgh, observed that 'There has been within recent years, a partial revival of one good old rule which, we trust, will become universal and perpetual—that no young person shall be admitted to the Lord's Table who cannot intelligently repeat the Belief, the Lord's Prayer, and the Ten Commandments.' Is this not a practice which, without being made obligatory, is worth pursuing?

I have made small reference to the act of confirmation. What is an encounter and confrontation of young people (and some older) with

45

their Master, and—who knows?—a turning-point in their lives demands a sense of occasion.

To you, the minister, as well as to them, it should be an occasion of immense significance and deep joy. Believing this, I would tell the confirmands at our final class meeting, 'I hope your parents will be there, and that you will invite your friends. After all, they will come on your wedding day! And this too is a milestone and, I hope, a great new beginning for you.

9 'O Taste and See'

In looking through the Communion Roll on one occasion I was surprised to find that Mrs E. had not attended for the four years since my induction. She was a friendly and happy member of the congregation and a tower of strength in the Sunday School, during whose holidays she attended church well. And now, the more rigid members of the Kirk Session informed me, we would have to consider purging her from the Roll! Since none of them could explain her absence from the Sacrament, I asked her directly. It was quite simple, she said; she stayed away because Communion Services depressed her. And she did not see any point in coming every three months to mourn the Saviour's death. I assured her that the service was no longer a depressing one—if it ever had been so; that it was far more than a memorial service; it was one of union with Christ; as Robert Bruce used to say 'at which we get a better grip of Him'. And also at which we are bound together in His love, and with all who love Him on earth and in heaven. I also told her how her withdrawal, when the whole family of the congregation met round the Table, was felt. (True, I had failed to miss her, but from the moment I realized her absence I was unhappy about it.) I am glad to say that she tried again and came to regard the occasion differently and to look forward to it.

There must be many who, without absenting themselves, think as she once did. And the Church is much to blame. We have been too afraid of sacrificing majesty, and have not seen that dignity can be loosened without being lost. One has only to look at the joyful celebration of the Mass in other countries and traditions. At a Corpus Christi Mass in Austria I was impressed by the solemnity of the observance, the silences, the tinkling bell, the reverence of the celebrants; but equally by the joyful hymns and the quiet happiness in the pews as families returned from the altar.

You will, of course, follow one of the Orders for the celebration of Holy Communion in the Service Book. So I need only add a few notes.

(a) To the Invitation, 'You who earnestly repent from your sins draw near and take this sacrament to your comfort and growth in grace' I have often added these words which I came upon many years ago in the late Dr Ernest Jarvis's Warrack Lectures:

Come, not because you are strong, but because you are weak. Not because any goodness of yours gives you the right to come, but because you need mercy and help.
Come because you love the Lord a little, and would like to love Him more. Come because He loves you, and gave Himself for you.
Lift up your hearts above all your cares, and let this bread and wine be to you the token and pledge of the grace of the Lord Jesus Christ, the love of God, and the Fellowship of the Holy Spirit. His grace be with you all.

(b) Christ Himself presides. He, and not the cup, is the Host. It is He who invites us, accepts us and feeds us. And so, when the minister speaks the words 'This is My body which is broken for you' he is the mouthpiece of the Lord Himself. This is a doctrine of the Real Presence, indeed, and far removed from the desiccated memorialism practised by Zwinglians and Arians. This is why the minister should himself partake of the Communion before he administers it. He should be the first to respond to the Lord's invitation. Unfortunately this has been misunderstood both by those ministers who serve the elders first and themselves last, and by the congregations which expect them to do so.

(c) The perfect ending to the service is surely one which contains words such as these, which appear in the 1980 Alternative Service Book of the Church of England:

Father of all, we give you thanks and praise, that when we were still far off you met us in your Son and brought us home. Dying and living, he declared your love, gave us grace, and opened the gate of glory. May we who share Christ's body live his risen life; we who drink his cup bring life to others; we whom the Spirit lights give light to the world.

(d) For the Blessing I would take neither 'The grace of the Lord Jesus Christ...' nor 'The peace of God...' for both have already been given. What could be more appropriate than 'The God of peace who brought again from the dead our Lord Jesus, that great Shepherd of the sheep, through the blood of the everlasting covenant, make you perfect in every good work to do His will (*or*, equip you with everything good, that you may do His will), working in you that which is pleasing (not the obsolete *well-pleasing*) in His sight, through Jesus Christ to whom be glory for ever and ever'? The risen Christ, the blood of the covenant, the work of salvation continuing in us, and the final *Gloria*; all this gathers up the very intent of the sacrament.

Part III
PASTORALIA

10 Getting to Know You

The minister deals with neither cases, clients nor customers. He deals with persons. And even the expression *deals with* rings false. When I visit the members of my own family and my friends I do not deal with them. I go just to enjoy their company; or to help them in a particular need; or because they want to see me.

This is the basis of all good pastoral work; a spontaneous interest in people, for themselves and not just as potential pew-fodder. I can only urge those who shrink from personal relationship and find the initiation of conversation terrifying, to take steps to overcome their diffidence.

But how? First by torpedoing that guilt-complex which tells you that because you have failed to converse to any purpose or indeed to say much at all, the visit was no good. What we say is of less importance than our friendship. Even a banal remark about the weather, or the simplest 'I'm glad to meet you' or 'How are all the family?' or, indeed, 'Have you a family?' is a breaker of the ice. Though warmth, rather than ice, is what you will meet. If, when you set out, you regard the enterprise not as a dutiful foot-slog, but as a chance to see people at closer quarters and get to know them better, you will not be disappointed.

The risk of being an unwelcome caller will be lessened by sensitive timing. If you know when your parishioners have their evening meal, you can avoid disrupting it. And with some it will be helpful to phone and say 'Will it suit you if I look in tomorrow, say around eight o'clock?'

Do not be too envious of ministers with a natural bonhomie. A facility for dropping in on people may only lead to perfunctory pastoral work—a cheery 'Hullo, how are you all?' then 'I must push along' and perhaps thirty or forty visits a week clocked up. But many people will not open up or unwind sufficiently in ten minutes, however soon you return for another brief encounter. The eye on the clock and the resolve to see another two that evening can stifle opportunities of counsel and comfort. There are some, of course, for whom ten minutes is enough. Not because they show no immediate interest or response—that may be a reason for cultivating them more—but the reverse; because you already know them so well that much of what you would say in other homes is taken for granted.

If there has been a turning away from the parish ministry—and that is disputable—it is sometimes attributed to the 'tea parties with old ladies' syndrome. Is it not effeminate for a red-blooded young man to spend his afternoons exchanging pleasantries in the parlour?

But there is another side to it. The majority of O.A.P.s happen to be female; consequently women predominate on our visiting lists. The minister has to relate to them and how better than over a cup of tea? Such visits reflect the Church's care. The exchanging of pleasantries may seem to little purpose, but it seldom stops there. The afternoons you spend in these homes will prove as rewarding as any. The pleasantries become conversation, which is something different; about their children and grandchildren, local events, news of the day, and all in the state of the world that is troubling them; also, of course, about their church, in the past and the present, and their concern for its future.

There are surprises too. Every life has its story. That bowed little body, whose life is so constricted, produces a medal and tells you of the days when she was Matron of a military hospital. Another, now half-blind, spent her active years teaching in Pakistan; her neighbour, arthritic and shuffling along on a zimmer, was a village schoolmistress with whom her pupils still correspond. A nonagenarian tells me of her pioneering days in Canada, and another how her fiancé was killed in the First War and so she went on working in the mill till she retired. Together they provide a mine of rich experience.

Counselling

When you visit you will uncover much more than the life-stories heard by the firesides of the aged and the housebound. You will come upon almost every case in the psychiatric book—personality disorders, phobias and anxieties, depressions and stresses, self-reproach and paranoia; also deep traumas caused by bereavement, marriage breakdown, catastrophic illness or serious accident. A downtown minister, on seeing one of Tennessee Williams' plays, told me that there was nothing there among the turbulent emotions, the disordered relationships and the fairly sordid ongoings , that he did not recognize as existing in his own parish!

51

Much of our pastoral work is obviously of a confidential nature and can only be discussed in general terms. You will find yourself dealing with situations which are deeply personal, often complicated and frequently delicate. There are the kind of problems the Catholic priest encounters in the confessional. There are marital problems. There are questions relating to elderly relatives; often the decision on whether to seek a place in sheltered housing or an eventide home. And the question of helping people to cope with ill-health, unemployment, or bereavement often in tragic circumstances. Less frequently, there are the kind of questions which the minister feels himself especially equipped to encounter (in contrast to those for which social workers, doctors and other professionals are trained); those that spring from spiritual longings, inner turmoil or religious doubts.

Psychological knowledge aids our understanding, but the practice of psychiatry is best left to the experts: and frequently our best contribution is to put someone in touch with an appropriate agency such as Marriage Guidance, A.A or a social worker, or with a doctor or lawyer. What we can do, which the experts with few exceptions cannot, is to pray with the sufferer or for him and to give spiritual assurance and the warmth of Christian love.

I seem to myself to have done far less counselling than all the contemporary discussion about it warrants. Maybe with some training I could have opened up more conversations that petered out and had access to more of the secret anxieties and problems that remained hidden. But might it not be that we exaggerate the number of problems that ordinary people have? Looking round now to my neighbours in the pews I wonder how many of them are troubled and in need of a counsellor? They need friends, and many have them, and a faith to live by and peace of heart, and they have that too. They need constantly to repent and grow in grace and always to thank the Lord—but to fulfil this is why they are there. But they are not conscious of needing additional counselling. Certainly only a handful ask for it; and this, I think, is good.

Counselling as we in the ministry practise it goes beyond the limitations which the professionals impose. According to the textbooks the counsellor has to be entirely non-judgmental; to look with an open mind at the 'client's' situation; and to help him to find his own solution. It is a lengthy process which begins with the building up of a relationship of trust. And it consists of non-intrusive sympathy rather than the giving of advice.

For the most part, however, we do not deal with 'clients'—i.e. people hitherto unknown to us. The relationship of trust, although it may still have to be built upon, is already there. And the problem posed may well be, what is the Christian way to take? To which it would be churlish to reply, You must work that out for yourself. There will be no ready-made solution, but there are Christian insights, standards and guidelines to which we can refer. Especially is this true in our premarriage counselling, when the couple may well want to know what Christian advice we have for them. While we are giving it we should not be 'laying it on the line' but at every turn asking 'Do you agree with this?' and 'What do you yourselves think about it?'

Those who seek our counsel may well include distraught parents whose refractory children have brought some disgrace upon the family, either by the daughter becoming pregnant or the son making someone else's daughter so; or by some escapade which has brought them into trouble with the police. The parents, especially if they are heavy-handed, may expect you to side entirely with them in their outrage, and in condemning the sins of their offspring; and may even be resentful if you do not share their feelings. But it is your duty in Christian compassion more than in judgment, to share the feelings of the young no less than of the old. 'When girls lost their virginity' says Monica Dickens, referring to a previous generation, 'it was often because they were too gauche to know how not to without losing face, which might be worse.' And in the greater sophistication of today this can still happen.

In the light of the Gospels I have always found the non-judgmental principle difficult. True, Jesus said, Judge not that you be not judged. And we should ever be aware that many of our judgments, and especially our condemnations are presumptuous, fallible and unnecessary. But when Jesus denounced the Pharisees, and when He said to the adulteress, Go and sin no more, was He not passing judgment? 'Well done, good and faithful servant' is no less a judgment than is 'Woe unto you'; 'that fox Herod' than 'You are not far from the kingdom of heaven'.

To tell people they are right, or good, or have done well—even to bolster their ego—may give the encouragement they need. To tell them they are wrong, or wicked, or have let someone down, may be salutary. And if we are to take our bearings from the New Testament—the Epistles no less than the Gospels—we will not hesitate both to praise and admonish, however non-committal our friends in more secular fields may choose to be.

Vestry Hour

Most city ministers have a vestry hour, when counselling, together with such items as signing passports, writing testimonials, greeting new members and transferring old ones take place. Baptisms, burials and beggars, appointments and resignations, weddings and forthcoming events are dealt with or arranged, as the case may be.

When there are no callers, the hour is a bonus in which to read, think, plan or pray. When there are many, I am always sorry for the pensioner with a form to fill, or the young person with a passport who is beaten in the queue by someone whose concern will occupy half-an-hour. So I suggest to any whom I know to be coming for a pre-Baptism or pre-marriage interview, or the repeat of a missed confirmation class that they should arrive towards the end of the hour, when I shall carry on; and to be willing to wait if there are short items to be disposed of. If the matter is a testimonial, however, and I have little knowledge of the person who asks for it, rather than dash off a dubious commendation I would say, 'Can I think this over and see what I can produce?' and take time to make further enquiries.

The most suitable hour for one's parishioners is, I think, 7-8; and for oneself the day when committees and meetings are least likely to occur. For me, this meant Thursday, and the fact that it was the night of the Choir Practice gave me opportunities to visit the choir. Being in mid-parish at 8 o'clock also meant that, if one was then free, there was a useful visiting-slot.

On the hoof

Counselling will also be done when we are just padding around the parish. Padding may be slow; but it is not the same as plodding. It simply means footwork, which is better than sticking to your car. Most ministers will admit that the days on which they left the car behind turned out to be rewarding. In your car you are inaccessible and there is always the feeling of missed opportunity as you pass someone you would like to have spoken to.

Degas is recorded as having said 'I don't like carriages. You don't see anyone. That's why I like the omnibus. You can always look at people. We are made to look at one another, aren't we?' Being an artist he just wanted to look. But ours is a closer engagement.

On the village street, and to a lesser extent in the urban parish, you make all sorts of casual encounters; and these are not as time-wasting as they may seem. Rather are they the seasons when we might, in Tennyson's phrase, 'take occasion by the hand'. Here's a chance to talk to that elusive chap who sits in the back pew, and slips away before I can catch him; or to ask Jessie for her mother; or to find out from Bob how the bowling match went last night; or to tell that young mum that we have begun a playgroup; or simply to say 'Hullo, how are you?'

Some of us rush around, as has been said, 'like super-charged scooters', but if people remark 'I can never catch him long enough to say what I want', it is energy wasted.

You will meet in the homes of your flock, as well as in more general visitation, the vast nonchurchgoing public, many of whom are indifferent or dismissive towards the Church or the local congregation, or critical of the Faith, or of yourself because you are a cleric. What they say you may have heard a hundred times, and since you do not expect to make any headway you refuse to be drawn; especially where it is apparent that an aggressive critic is in the grip of a neurosis is it futile to pursue reasoned argument. It might be well, however, to heed the advice of St Paul in words which the Jerusalem Bible translates thus: 'Be tactful with those who are not Christians and be sure you make the best use of your time with them. Talk to them agreeably and with a flavour of wit, and try to fit your answers to the needs of each one.' (Col 4.5-6). They may be echoing parrot-cries but they are more than parrots; people with needs which make them react in that particular way.

The awkward squad

There are nutters and cranks; bees in their bonnets and chips on their shoulders. Some with a crush on the minister and others who suspect him of heresy. The humourless and ultra-pietistic; the over-sensitive, easily hurt or quick to take offence; the groaners and the compulsive talkers; young firebrands whom you disappoint by not endorsing their radicalism, and grim old diehards who oppose all change. 'You name 'em, we've got 'em'.

By their very oddity, of manner or of opinion, they have become isolated and alienated from normal friendships, and should be given, at the very least, tolerance and kindness, even if one has to be careful not to encourage their too frequent attentions. Among those with whom you are eager to relate are some who make it difficult. Such as the compulsive talkers, who are apt to accost you at some moment when you should be elsewhere. This is irksome, but what are you to do? To curb the flow abruptly with a sharp interjection may not only offend but hurt them as well. The only expedient is to anticipate the crux of their spiel and, by a judicious question, bring them there more speedily; then, if you can take over the talking for a moment, pick up your hat and flee!

Visiting, unprogrammed and selective

'Is it a convenient moment?' How often have I said this on someone's doorstep. It gives them the chance to say 'Well as a matter of fact we've got visitors'; or 'Well, we're at our supper' or perhaps nowadays 'We're just showing a film on video'. In such cases a strategic withdrawal may pay the dividend of a more satisfactory visit next time, when your considerateness will be remembered. And even where everything seems propitious to ask 'Is it a convenient moment?' is to show courtesy.

'And Abraham went out not knowing whither he went.' That is one way in which to go visiting. Not that all our visits should be unprogrammed; but when we are jaded with routine a sally into the unknown can be revivifying. You decide to turn north, and under a lamppost consult your pocket rollbook, 'Who is there around here? Ah, yes, the Maloneys—time I saw them... Mrs Gray, but she'll be at the Young Mums tonight... The Hopes—that lass who teaches in the Primary is a Hope and has a brother, but I don't know them all... Drummond—rings no bell, but I may know the face... and Mrs Green, but she's old and I'll get her in the afternoon.'

Unscheduled calls here and there bring to the congregation a feeling that they are cared for near and far; and those in District 20 do not feel that they will have to wait until nineteen districts have been covered before you reach them.

Methodical visiting gives the assurance that the minister is on the job. The inevitable drawback is that if he promises to be in Dudley Crescent on Tuesday evening people will feel obliged to wait in; and if he is held up, or does not reach Mrs X until 9.30, she will feel 'I could have been at the Rural after all.' But one can be methodical without making a definite commitment; chancing the shut door and being prepared to call again.

Selective visiting is the most useful of all. 'The tinker goes where the kettles need mending.' Yes, but how do you know? Either word gets around (and it is often inaccurate) or you must already have a thorough knowledge of your area. If you have visited the whole congregation, and if possible the parish, you will have acquired a shrewd idea of where you are needed. And it will not be only by the sick and the housebound. Here is a lonely widower, or a widow who has become self-pitying and solitary; a family dogged with ill-luck, or with delinquent youngsters; a mother who longs to be in contact with the church but with a young brood to care for; a boy or girl leaving high school who has no prospect of a job or cannot decide what to do, another who has crashed in his exams. An incomer whom nobody wants to know...

'When I was in hospital the minister never called on me.' In spite of the good work of hospital chaplains in notifying ministers, this complaint is frequently heard. The minister may be blameworthy, through carelessness or a lapse of memory. The failure to make contact, however, is usually due to a breakdown in communication. The grapevine has not worked. Someone has thought that someone else would tell you. However well he knows his parishioners the minister will not always be informed of their up-to-the-minute state of well-being. He can take certain measures to remedy this. He can emphasize to church workers that they should bring any such case to his notice; and make a similar request to the whole congregation. He can ask the local doctor and district nurse to tell him, if they are willing, of anyone they think he should visit. And there are other individuals, especially in a small community, who are prime sources of information: in my rural parish those whom I consulted, when I returned from holiday, included the ambulance driver, the postmistress and a member who served in the busy grocer's shop. Between them they brought me up to date on the pastoral situation.

To pray or not to pray?
To conduct worship in anyone's home without a by-your-leave is, I believe, wrong. The minister, like any other welcomed visitor, is a guest and must not take over. On the other hand we should ask in many more homes than we do, 'Would you like a prayer?' or 'Could we have a reading and a prayer before I go?' It may be deeply appreciated, nowhere more than in some of the homes where we have been hesitant to suggest it.

A pocket Bible—or sometimes a Psalter or Gospel—is better than the conspicuous one which suggests a predetermined resolve. I would wish people to think 'He has come to see me,' rather than 'He has come to pray'. We visit out of love, and it is when a loving relationship has been established that we can best pray together. But if the relationship is not already there we must take time to establish it— and among 'fringe' members this takes longer, perhaps many visits before you venture to pray.

Even with the sick and the housebound I usually ask before I pray. For 'Do you feel like a prayer today?' is sometimes met with 'No thank you—I'm rather tired—next time if you don't mind'. We do not always realise how exhausted the sick can be, and even to concentrate on the minister's words (which should be very brief) may require effort. I usually ask: but there are some who do not have to be asked. You have often prayed together, and they expect it. These, too, in time of illness feel exhaustion. And when I discern that they are anxious lest I stay too long or are trying to hide physical discomfort, or are hoping that I will not assume that they are wanting me to read and pray, I might say 'Just a blessing today, for you're tired. "The Lord bless you and keep you ..."'; and, perhaps, with hand on hand, or laid on their head.

The parish pub

As a parish minister I often asked myself what I should do about the pubs and I decided that they were not my scene so I had better stay away. To go there frequently would be to make a false profession (which is also why I did not assume an ardour for the Freemasons or even the Bowling Club); to go infrequently would suggest that I was trying to exercise my ministry, rather than being sociable like everyone else. So I stayed away and met most of the pub's clientele in their own homes. But I did not regard the pub as a kind of purdah; nor hesitate to go in (off-hours) to visit the publican and his family or (on-hours) to look for someone, or pass a message to the barmaid who was, when her duties permitted, a youth club leader.

Beyond the fold—those of other faiths

Living in a multi-racial society we are more than likely in our parish visitation, especially in the inner city, to encounter Pakistanis or Sikhs, Chinese or Hindus. What shall we, or any other visitors from the congregation, say when they open the door? It is no use mentioning parish visitation or the parish church: they won't have a clue. My approach would be something like this. 'We are from the church round the corner, and we're just making a friendly call. Are you happy in Edinburgh (or wherever) and is there anything we can do for you?' If they continued the conversation, I might ask if they knew about the Women's International Centre (or the International Flats in Glasgow or Dundee). I might also say, 'I expect you have your own place of worship?' and, if they are devout, 'Tell me about it: what happens there?' There might also be an opportunity to invite their children to playgroup or Brownies, or themselves to some social activities.

The keynote is friendship. Any attempt to proselytise is misguided. Believing, as we do, that Christ is the Saviour of mankind, the fulfilment of Hinduism and the crown of Islam, we may in our hearts want to say to them, as Paul did to Agrippa: 'I would to God that you were as I am.' But that cannot be said until we have tried to stand in their shoes, and appreciate their religion from the inside; and have regarded them not as unenlightened but, unless they be atheists, as sharing in the light of the knowledge of God, over against the darkness of materialism, even though they have not seen His glory in the face of Christ Jesus.

The Church's task, with these ethnic minorities, is, in the first place, to build bridges of friendship and understanding. That task, like the ecumenical one, must be carried out locally; where the parish churches, led by their ministers, have an inescapable part to play.

Beyond the fold—the lapsed and the outsiders

It is apparent that there are no limits to those whom the minister should visit; and among such variegated demands he will ask himself where the priorities lie. Certainly as I have said 'the tinker goes where the kettles need mending'. But there is something more, a word of Jesus which we cannot forget: 'If one of you has a hundred sheep and loses one of them, does he not leave the ninety-nine in the open pasture and go after the missing one until he has found it?'

In the light of that saying, our priority is the man or woman whose name is on the church roll, but who is no longer with us: who has wandered off and ceased to care. When the roll is revised and his name discovered the district elder says, 'He just is not interested', and the others may say, 'Let's take him off'. At that point, if not before it, the minister should chip in 'Let me go and see him'. In fact, we ought to know about such people even before they are blacklisted. And if we

59

spend time with them no one need accuse us of not visiting the congregation for they too are the congregation, though estranged. At the end of the day we may not have restored them to the fold, but we will at least have tried; and shown them that if they do not care, Christ and His Church do, and though they compel us to rescind their membership we long to welcome them back again.

The Church's mission starts right here. But it is also possible to spend so much time on strayed sheep who have no intention of returning that there is none left for less hopeless outsiders; that vast company of kind and friendly people who are mentally alive and full of good works, often highly gifted and endowed with qualities which the Church needs—but who, through some quirk of upbringing, have passed it by. To reach them is an irrefutable and crucial task; and one that cannot await the sporadic forays which usually express the Church's outreach. To get to know such people and, when the time is opportune, to bring to them the claims of Christ and His Church should, I believe, have a higher pastoral priority than it has yet been given.

Whether we can be bothered to do this is a test of our pastoral spirit. Forgiveness is a Christian virtue which we even tediously proclaim. But some of us find it easier to forgive people than to be bothered with them, quirks, warts and all. Bothering, listening, being available is what pastoral work is all about.

11 Bedside Manners

Ministers are warmly welcomed at most hospitals, but the staff prefer that they avoid rest hours, meal times and normal visiting hours. They should also be prepared to wait outside if there is a good reason.

Before visiting the patient we should see the sister or the nurse in charge; ask if it is convenient and enquire, 'How is he today?' The response is invariably helpful. No doctor would go into a ward without first consulting the sister and when a member of the staff is available, as is usually the case, we should do likewise. To do otherwise is to 'pull rank' and to convey an air of self-importance. The staff will resent this.

And now, when you get to the sick bed, what do you do? Certainly nothing by rote. Your words and actions will be determined by who the patients are, and by an assessment of their need in which you will often—maybe always—find you are guided by the Holy Spirit.

There are no rules about the length of a visit. We should be sensitive to the patient's reaction. If you sense that he is getting restless you have overstayed. In long-term wards you can generally stay longer. We should also gauge sensitively when, or indeed whether, to offer a moment of worship. Verses from a Psalm, perhaps, or 'This is part of what we read in church on Sunday,' and a brief prayer or sometimes just a blessing.

Doctors, nurses, and ministers must be open to the feelings of the patient about himself, and try to relate to him at the point where he is. It may be that he will want to be left alone with his own thoughts, and this spiritual privacy should not be invaded. There is a process of disengagement from this world which is painful and which he may want to endure silently. In the contemplation of death itself and of the life beyond death, there is also a privacy which we should respect.

In every large hospital there are those without relatives or friends. A caring minister and congregation can be invaluable here. Sometimes the Chaplain and staff uncover such situations; or church visitors, looking in at visiting hours, discern the unvisited.

In his poem 'Ten Types of Hospital Visitor' Charles Causley humorously sketches various attitudes to the sick and how the patients are likely to react.

The sixth visitor says little,
Breathes reassurance,
Smiles securely. (*Collected Poems 1971-2000*, Macmillan)

Ward services

A diminishing number of hospitals have ward services. There is, how-ever, a case for the ward service. There are those who are able to worship though unable to leave their bedside. And among those who would not openly identify with us are many who are interested in what is going on, and do not feel imposed upon. The hospital authorities will select the ward; and will steer clear of any with very ill, or in any way disturbed, patients. And anyone who objects to the service can have temporary refuge in a side ward. But even those who do not ac-cept a hymnbook nor take part in the prayers often appreciate the friendliness of the visitors and, to put it at its lowest, the break from routine. Provided, of course, that nothing is over-long, or too demand-ing or emotional. What is called for is two or three well-known hymns, perhaps abbreviated—but not always the 23rd Psalm, *What a Friend we have in Jesus*, *The Day Thou Gavest* and *Abide with Me*!—a short prayer or two, including thanksgiving and intercession, a Bible pass-age of not more than ten verses and a few comments thereon.

The emphasis should not be entirely on personal religion. The prime need may well be to be taken out of themselves and to hear of the faith of others and of the Gospel in the world. But inevitably there is a personal element in the prayers. When we pray for any who cannot sleep, or are lonely, or face an operation, we will be articulating felt longings and some will be strengthened by these prayers. They will also welcome the chance to pray for their loved ones whom we should never fail to mention.

Communion

Members of the Church of Scotland may not ask for it frequently but when it is offered it is often accepted, and arrangements to dispense it are easily made. The screens can be drawn round the bed; or use be made of a day-room or side ward where others may also wish to come. And it need not always be the parish minister who celebrates. The hospital chaplain may be able to do so more easily, and will certainly be willing if the patient is happy to have him; and we may be able to initiate this.

12 Binding the Brokenhearted

Even if you are inexperienced in funerals, you will before long come up against the problem of how not to let your feelings become blunted. When you have repeated the same words for the hundredth time, and sung the 23rd Psalm and *Abide with Me* only less often than the crematorium organists have to play them, how can you not grow stale; and the whole business, so full of loving, sorrowful emotion for everyone else, become for you just a routine? Only by the freshness of your spirit. By your own silent prayers for the mourners. By thinking not only of what you must do, but of them. By looking again at familiar words and by a certain extemporaneity in the phrasing of the prayers and the selection of passages, even of verses within a passage, so that you do not do exactly as you have done before. Also, of course, by finding out, as you visit the bereaved, features of the life and character of those whom you bury, and of the state of mind, presence or absence of faith, of their friends so that the whole service is *sui generis* and right for the occasion. A funeral, it has been said, should be a heart-warming, loving experience. I agree.

There are those who deliberately avoid the personal: they believe it should be transcended, and the thoughts of the mourners directed away from their loss to the great objective facts of the faith. These should indeed be dominant—the victory of the Cross and Resurrection, the communion of saints, and the life everlasting. But there is always a place for grateful recollection; thanks for all that the life, the love and the friendship given on earth has meant to one and another present; and surely we can tell God that 'our love and our prayers follow him' and ask Him 'to continue in heaven the good work You began in him here on earth.' Nor need we forbear to hope not only for a general resurrection but also for a day of reunion 'when the clouds will break and all earth's shadows flee away.'

An agnostic explained why she wanted a church funeral for her husband. 'He would want his friends to say goodbye to him in dignity and fellowship.' It was a true insight. It is not only a Christian ordinance, but also a human valediction and a gathering together of people who may not all share in our fellowship in Christ, but who are sensible of their fellowship in love for their friend. To acknowledge such feelings is not the least of our obligations.

It is all very well to think 'Nothing is here for tears', but in all but a few rare cases there is someone who feels the sorrow of parting and the emptiness of loss. At such a time we have to 'sit where they sit'. The mourning may be neither acute nor unduly melancholy; but it will be a gentle undercurrent. I say this because in our anxiety to proclaim the gospel of the resurrection we can be inconsiderate. The old lady has died at last. Ah well, she is with Christ, which is far better, and all is joy. But even in the gentlest bereavement the buoyancy of our faith must be tempered with understanding.

Still more is sensitivity needed when the death is tragic or premature. Here the danger is the opposite one of so entering into the heartbreak that you cannot raise anyone above it. Many a funeral is a sad, sad occasion, with the friends and relatives at breaking point. Very possibly they are looking desperately to you for some word of comfort; you are to be the rock on which they lean. Christ is the rock, as you know; but it is often through you that He will come to them.

But no funeral should be lugubrious. A point made by Stan Laurel when he said: 'If anyone at my funeral has a long face, I'll never speak to them again.' Yet many funerals are bleak and gloomy.

Since, as my old professor, Hugh Mackintosh, used to say, 'There is more in Christ to make us glad than there can be anywhere else to make us sorry,' this is a betrayal of the faith. The minister's role is surely both to mourn with those who mourn and to rejoice in the unquenchable hope of the gospel. He has to articulate grief for many who are dumb with sorrow; but he has also to articulate the Easter faith. And because at every funeral there are mourners to whom that faith means nothing, one prays that one may not miss the evangelical opportunity; not by intruding any note of preaching or using the funeral for ends other than its own, but simply by being 'in the Spirit' and dwelling in Christ and in the dimension of the world unseen.

At the main service one has to decide whether the readings should be one or two of a reasonable length or several which are brief. On the whole I have erred by being too 'bitty', there being so many 'comfortable words' that one is tempted to include too much. There are also such passages as Psalm 121, John 14, Romans 8, 1Cor 15, 2Cor 4 and Revelation 21—all magnificent but obviously one cannot read them all. No, but one can prune and compress, and for example read the first four verses of Psalm 23 and/or the last four of Psalm 121.

The passage from John 14 is already a compression, so it is not sacrilegious to prune it again and go from 'that where I am, there ye may be also' to 'Peace I leave with you.' I always speak our Lord's words from memory. When no book comes between, they spring to life in a new way and bear comfort to the hearers.

There are other words not in the service books which I have frequently included. That great sentence from the Apocrypha—'The faithful shall abide with Him in love; the care of them is with the most High'. And from Isaiah—'When thou passest through the waters I will be with thee; and through the rivers they shall not overflow thee.' Is it not also extraordinary that we are not given 'Eye hath not seen, nor ear heard, neither have entered into the heart of man, the things which God hath prepared for them that love Him'?

The committal can be a moment of trust and hope, and a quiet affirmation of faith in the lifegiving God. The keynote should certainly be neither 'Man goes to his long rest' nor 'Prepare to meet your God' but, rather, 'Underneath are the everlasting arms'.

When the funeral is over—vamoose! Shake hands, say you will be in touch, and go. They will invite you to a meal, but unless they are insistent make your excuses. You will not be missed among the shared memories and family reunions.

It is in the weeks and months which follow, when friends and neighbours have departed, that your support, and the congregation's, is most needed. Anyone who knows the first thing about bereavement is aware that a year is a short time in which to recover from the initial grief, the onsets of loneliness and misery, the enfeebled will and the sense that the mainspring has gone out of living. During this time not only should the local congregation rally round, but in an especial way the minister. Some, I know, note in their diaries the anniversary of the death and pay then a much-appreciated call. But all through the time of acute grief our friendship and what we stand for can provide spiritual therapy; our prayers, if they be quiet and positive, bring healing; and our confidence, born of seeing so many folk come through sorrow and begin life again, beget hope.

Two postscripts. In the distress of bereavement people are easily persuaded by well-meaning friends, or by the undertaker, to say 'No letters please'. This is a mistaken kindness, for letters bring great comfort. I found this for myself when my first wife died. When her friends wrote to say what a wonderful person she was, when they recalled incidents and encounters that I had forgotten, or revealed how much some act or word had meant to them, I found it not only touching but deeply consoling; as was the faith that also shone through their letters. So I take every opportunity to advise people not to deprive themselves of this consolation. And I add how good it is for the letter-writers as well, that they should be able to express their love.

After a funeral the minister may receive a 'perk' in the form of a cheque. Is he to retain this for himself or to give it to the church? There is no general rule. On one occasion I receive £10 and pass it on to the Treasurer; on another I buy religious books or some other item that will contribute to my ministry; and on a third I use it freely. The first of these perks may come from a non-churchgoer whom I hardly know. It is not so much a personal gift as a donation (or even conscience money) to the church. The second may be from someone who has come from another parish or place to bury their parent. Since there is doubt as to whether it is for me or for the church, I compromise by restricting its use. The third is from a family whom I know well and who are obviously expressing their gratitude not just for the funeral but for my care for their loved one over the years. Although all my visits, perhaps to a distant hospital, were no more than my duty, I know that they intend this gift for me—were it for the church they had known how to give it there—so I use it as they intend. It is all a matter of sensitivity.

13 'To Love and to Cherish'

Weddings would become tedious if it were not for the people. The procedure is repetitious down to the cold salad and trifle and the greetings (not always tasteful) read at the reception. Even the service can pall—'Beloved, we have come together... Marriage is appointed that there may be... I am required to ask... if you know any reason...' Then there is 'O perfect love'—though mercifully less habitual now that the old tune is more inaccessible. And afterwards, the long-winded photographer and the extensive interludes of non-activity.

So what is one to do? There is only one answer: think of and for the people. Rejoice with them that rejoice. Enter into the feelings of the young couple and of their families. And when at the end of the bridal table you find yourself immolated for an hour with the bride-groom's grannie or the youngest bridesmaid, put yourself out for them, and try to contribute to their day.

Above all, while you say the prayers hold in your mind the image of this particular couple, this unique family, so that you are not only reiterating words but praying for those who are there before you.

But now we must go back in time. Some months before the pro-posed date a couple will tell you they want a church wedding. 'We'd like Saturday the 8th of March at 2 o'clock.' You have little room for manoeuvre for they have already procured a hall for the Reception. In springtime especially these have to be booked early. So you refrain from telling them you had hoped to be at the Welsh match at Murray-field on that date, and comply. Not before ascertaining, however—if they are unknown to you—what the circumstances are, and why they want a church wedding. Probably all is well; there is no dubious divorce, elopement, under-age barrier, possibility of bigamy or other hindrance. And they prefer the church, not merely for show but be-cause, in an inarticulate way, they believe it is the right place. A con-viction you will endorse by telling them that it is indeed so, for a marriage which acknowledges the Presence of God and in which thanks are given and vows paid to Him carries more meaning than one at the Registrar's in which vows are made only to one another.

You will, you explain, be talking with them about marriage at your next meeting, but at this early stage you will simply book the date, and tell them anything they need to know about the procedure. For instance, where to find the registrar and how soon to see him. Also that they must choose the hymns, for printing, in good time; a task in which they may welcome advice. They should also know that many stationers can provide these 'off the peg' but how limited their selection is likely to be. (Produce samples if you can.) They may also, at this stage, like to know what costs are entailed. The Kirk Session will have fixed these, and should revise them from time to time; the essential items being fees for the organist and the church officer and a donation towards church heating; the summer fees contributing to the winter's warmth. They may enquire about a fee for the minister, and the answer is that there is none.

Two or three weeks before the wedding-day you should see the couple again. 'After the first hymn,' I tell them, 'you will hear me read something about marriage from the service book. It says that marriage is 'appointed' ('ordained' in the older book) for four purposes. I'll tell you what it says: but, first, I wonder if *you* can tell *me*—what would you say the first purpose of marriage is? In other words, why are you getting married?' The answer is usually 'Because we love one another', but sometimes they say 'To have a family'. To the former I reply 'Of course. And that is what the book says. It speaks of the companionship, comfort and joy between husband and wife. And if you aren't going to give these to each other, you should call the whole thing off.' We then go on to discuss companionship and all that it means. That neither has rights over the other but that all things, both mundane and spiritual should be shared. Shared activities and mutual interests in the home and outside it; and being interested not only in one another but in the larger world. Shared ideals and openness to one another; openness about money; concern about each other's work; encouragement of each other's religious faith; the planning of many things together, from where to go for holidays to when to have a family, and how many to have.

'And that leads on,' I would say, 'to another of the purposes of marriage—"It is appointed for the ordering of family life".' If however, the couple have already said that the first purpose of marriage is to have a family, I will have pointed out that that only comes first in the older service books (and came first, surprisingly, at Prince Charles's wedding). But that now we have a more balanced view, and realize that even if you are unfortunate and cannot have children your marriage is not a failure—for the first purpose is the loving companionship. 'To have a family' is here in the service because it is indeed one of the purposes but it is not the first one.

The service refers to children as 'God's gifts to us'. (The older books spoke of 'the holy ordinance of family life' and children as 'the heritage of the Lord'). This is not just religion being tagged on. For when you think of the word 'procreation' it means more than begetting or giving birth. It means that we act 'pro'—on behalf of—the Creator. We are not only propagating our own species, but doing God's work, bringing into the world a creature of His. Animals propagate their own kind but only men and women can produce a child of God. And whenever we baptize a baby that is what we are saying, that he is not only a son of Adam, but a child of God. Therefore every child should be a wanted child and be given, as the book says, 'the security of love and the heritage of faith'.

'We've spent some time on children,' I might add, 'and that's all in the future: but it's as well to think what you are heading for. However, let's get back to *now*.' The service still has more to say about marriage. There is the physical side. 'It is appointed as the right and proper setting for the full expression of physical love...' And the social side: 'for the well-being of human society'. Both of these facets may provoke discussion.

The first puts sex in its true perspective, as the expression of a personal relationship; not merely a physical instinct. The Christian view, I would stress, is by no means repressive nor anti-sex. Sex is a God-given instinct to be used as an expression of love. But it can be abused. For instance, when a man treats a woman as a thing to be used rather than as a person to be loved—and that can occur in marriage as well as out of it. The distinction between love and lust is surely that lust only wants to take while love also wants to give. And the great thing in marriage is to cherish one another—a lovely word which means to treasure, to care for, and to serve. (Another expressive word is 'cleave'.)

Finally there's the social side. 'What you are doing,' I would say, 'doesn't only affect yourselves. You are creating a new cell in the body politic. If it is a successful marriage others will benefit, and society be all the more stable: if it breaks down, society will have to pick up the bits, perhaps even through a psychiatric hospital, and there may be children, whose world has broken down, to rescue.'

I would urge them to be concerned about the larger world, not to retreat into their own private castle. And tell them that 'the well-being of human society' also means that where marriage-standards are low, where there is unfaithfulness, fornication and a too high divorce-rate, the moral fibre of society is sapped. Did this factor not contribute to the collapse of Imperial Rome? And appeal to them not to leave their parents out in the cold— 'You don't want them living on top of you, but you should make them feel that they haven't entirely lost you; that they and you are inside the larger family circle.'

On, then, to the wedding-day. When you arrive the ushers will already be there; and they may well ask if they have got the seating right—on which side do the bride's people sit? The answer, of course, is behind the bride; i.e. to the minister's right. I have seen some village ushers start off wrongly and have to have an early general post! You then find in the vestry two rather similar and nervous young men who have arrived early. Having forborne to say 'No smoking, please' and found a makeshift ashtray, you determine which is the bridegroom. You had interviewed him the other day, but spruced up and with his hair groomed it could be the other chap! Having sorted this one out you ask for the schedule (or produce it) and to save time fill in all but the signatures required later. When word comes that the bride is arriving you take your wards into the church and yourself go back or forward, as the case may be, to welcome and lead her in. As her father moves into the pew you slip him a hymnsheet, without which he will probably have to share one, and you also have copies for those, including the bridesmaids, who stand before you. You recoup these from the three principals after the first hymn and return them when required. You will also have told the bride to pass any bouquet, gloves, etc. to her bridesmaid.

Presently we are at the Vows, and you will have checked in the vestry which version it will be. (*They* will not have forgotten what was decided some weeks ago, but *you* well may.) If they have chosen to repeat the words rather than to say 'I do', you should judge their capacity for taking a whole clause, or simply a phrase, at a time. A variant used by many, including myself, is 'as long as we both shall live' for 'until God shall separate us by death'. For the latter may unwittingly give the impression of a final severance not of the marital status only but of a relationship which, if it be true and loving, is eternal; whereas the former carries an overtone of 'for ever and ever'. For a bridegroom who wished to say something at the giving of the ring, I willingly inserted, 'With this ring I thee wed; with my body I thee honour; and all my worldly goods with thee I share.'

The service book places the Address before the Scripture Reading, but there are occasions when one wants to comment on a passage that has been read. For instance I might read 'And Ruth said: Whither thou goest I will go; and where thou lodgest I will lodge; thy people shall be my people, and thy God my God.' (Verses which, surprisingly, are not in the Lectionary.) I would then want to say 'This bonnie tale speaks to us today. Ruth, like both of you, set out for a new country, a new way of life. You are saying to each other what she said to Naomi—committing yourself to the other. In doing so you give up your independence, but in losing you find—far more... Her people will be yours, and yours hers. You will enrich their lives, and they yours. And you will share your faith in God: this, and serving Him, will give deep meaning and purpose to your life together...'

And now comes the Reception where, when you are not out on a limb, you may have to be the unofficial MC. No one else is likely to 'chair' the speeches or to advise the best man when, and how, to read the greetings. (You will, prior to the event, have explained, should they not know it, that the bridegroom toasts the bridesmaids and the best man replies on their behalf.) It will not come amiss if you urge the best man to speak up and to identify Jack and Sue, who have sent a message, as the bride's Canadian cousins or Jimmy and the Lads as the bridegroom's workmates.

On innumerable occasions you will be asked to toast the bride and bridegroom. You will be expected to enliven the proceedings with native wit or with a story or two. Remember, though, that your role is not merely to provide a comic turn. You should begin by saying something graceful, or grateful, about the occasion and end by expressing the loving wishes of the guests. Moreover, better than 'gags' or stories are the lighthearted remarks which emerge from your own knowledge of the pair, or from data acquired on the spot from their friends and relations.

When the guests have risen from table, you may be able to say farewell and go. But if there is not too long a hiatus it is better to wait until the dancing begins. Then, having enjoyed the bridal waltz and participated briefly in this part of the celebration, either on the floor or as an onlooker, you can decently withdraw.

A minister was asked to remarry a couple both of whom had been divorced. After talking with them and learning of the tragedy of their previous marriages, (they were the 'innocent parties' but were quick to acknowledge their share of blame), of their concern for their

71

children, and their desire to make a new start (which included transferring their church affiliation to a new district) he said this: 'How privileged I felt that these fine people had come to me, and had asked this church to help them.'

The more doubtful marriages are those involving teenagers, or a teenage girl and an older man, who are flouting the wishes of parents. They may be right or wrong, and the minister is seldom able to judge. If he knows the parents better than the young people, and has seen their distress he will be tempted to take their part; but unless he has also come to know the youngsters and to be convinced that they are irresponsible he must not be partisan. Nor is it enough, where there is doubt, simply to refuse to marry them: if their minds are made up they will only go elsewhere. The best way is surely to give such counsel as you can about the nature of marriage, and about the family relationship which must some day—after the marriage if it is not possible beforehand—be repaired.

They will probably tell you that they know what they are doing. The only answer to this is to discuss their plans, if any, for the future. What do they intend to do about a house, about their jobs and about starting or deferring a family? And what are the pros and cons of the latter? What, especially, is their idea of love? Is it just that they like to be together, or is there a real element of cherishing and giving, with a willingness on both sides to make sacrifices and share responsibilities?

Finally, when the newly-weds, whether they have a church connection or not, live in the parish, you should drop in, a few weeks later, to see them and admire their home. Not only is this appreciated, but it shows them that the warmth of your feelings towards them at the wedding was not assumed for the occasion but still continues. And though no word is said on their attitude towards the Church they may, when you have gone, decide to do something about it.

14 'A meeting will be held...'

A parish minister is, quite literally, a chairperson. It is a part of the role. For scarcely a week passes without your having to preside at a meeting.

So what happens at a Session meeting? First of all, it is 'constituted by prayer'. What an incongruous phrase! Prayer is a man addressing his Maker not an administrative mechanism. However, at the end of the prayer the statutory words are said: 'We now constitute this meeting of a Court of the Church, in the name of Him who is its King and Head, Jesus Christ, to whom be glory for ever.'

But what goes before these words? What kind of prayer? There is no stereotype. An invocation of the Holy Spirit, asking for His vision and guidance is appropriate. So also is a pastoral prayer; the minister and elders interceding for the congregation, for its leaders, for the homes the elders visit and for individuals known to be in need. Or it may be a prayer for the matters in hand or for any immediate congregational concern. Or for the parish. Or for some public event—an election, a strike, a national crisis, or disaster—some concern that is in everyone's mind.

After the prayer, does one immediately get down to business, or set aside a brief period for Bible study, or for the presentation of, or discussion on, some topic of importance to the Church? Valuable though this be, it is not always acceptable. When I suggested it to one Kirk Session an elder said 'We're all busy men here, Mr Levison'; implying that while *I* might have time for such things as Bible study, *they* certainly did not! Other Sessions have achieved it—either at the beginning or end of their proceedings—and an increasing number have gone further and found the value of an occasional non-statutory meeting, a day-conference, or a weekend visit to a Church centre. Ventures highly to be recommended. I especially like the Session which has formed a tradition of holding a different kind of meeting once a quarter. They begin with a meal, then repair to business and end with Communion: the washing-up forming a suitable epilogue. There is a real deepening of fellowship there.

And now to the business. There are several ways of conducting it, and not all ministers are effective chairmen. You can race through the agenda, disallowing discussion and coming to peremptory decisions; or you can let all argue to their hearts' content. You can select the major items and spend such an inordinate time on them that the rest have to go by the board. Or you can deal so thoroughly with items of lesser moment which happen to come early on the agenda that important affairs get short shrift. I recall one minister, friendly and charming off duty, who used to chair the meetings of an Assembly committee with an efficiency marred by a caustic tongue; and in whose presence the less bold would forbear to say their say lest they be smacked down.

To be dismissive and to dither are equally bad. The ideal chairman will come to the meeting after carefully examining the agenda. He will give due time to every item; which means looking ahead, and maybe tightening the reins with 'There are three important matters still to come.' He will encourage members to speak, be firm with those who digress, try to curb the garrulous, and defuse the remarks of the truculent. He will give a lead, or express an opinion when he deems that such is required. He will solicit the opinions of the more recent, the younger and the diffident members. He will preserve an unruffled courtesy and calm, especially when a discussion becomes acrimonious. Above all he will not dominate, but will respect and listen to the opinions of others, whether he agrees with them or not. He will know that his is an advantageous position inasmuch as on ecclesiastical matters the elders are conscious of being less well-informed. He will not use this advantage to promote his partialities or spread his antipathies; nor cursorily dismiss any matter referred from Assembly or Presbytery. For it is not always conservatism in the eldership that impedes progress and growth. Ministers exerting their *episcope* have brought to a halt many a promising development.

The only sphere in which the minister sometimes has to insist on having his way is that indicated in the Church's Constitution: 'The ministry of the Word, the conduct of public worship, the dispensing of the Sacraments, and the instruction of the young belong to the minister, subject to the control and direction of the Presbytery' (J.T. Cox, *Practice and Procedure in the Church of Scotland*, 4th Ed., p.51). Even here it is best to consult the Session and, if possible, to obtain their agreement.

Few meetings are of equal importance to that at which the Kirk Session discusses the election of new elders. It is better that this should not take place immediately after an induction, but that the new minister be given time to know people and to assess the possible nominees. Once the number of elders required has been determined a decision on the method of election is taken. Of the authorised methods described in *Practice and Procedure* the most popular is that of resolution by the Kirk Session. Certainly in a large congregation the alternative methods of nomination and voting by the congregation are less suitable; there being a fair chance of the worthy being overlooked and the less worthy being nominated by their friends.

There are, of course, other types of meeting. You may have to chair anything from a Burns Supper to a Brains Trust. You must know when to be serious, when light-hearted and relaxed. It is for the chairman to set the tone and express the mood. And when it comes to introductions and votes of thanks, you must be neither longwinded nor fulsome, nor must you trespass on the speaker's subject before he gets there himself. The timing of the meeting is also in your hands, where neither a late start, unnecessary intervals, nor a lengthy finale should detract from an evening's programme. Adequate time for questions and discussion is often denied to a speaker and his audience, either because of poor planning—the insertion, for instance, of unnecessary preliminary items—and a programme that runs behind schedule; or through misjudgment by the chairman who forecloses the discussion sooner than everyone else would wish. If the give and take is valuable and going well, is it not better to cut out the closing hymn and end with a short prayer?

Part IV
THE FLOCK

15 Fostering Fellowship

To care for the flock, to foster and feed them, and to enable them more and more to become a living fellowship, a family of the people of God, is a paramount task; and to care also, as Jesus made plain, for the sheep that have strayed.

But who comprise the flock? Without an orderly and up-to-date church roll it is impossible to tell; for there are more than those whom you will meet on a Sunday. A roll with a minimum of erroneous addresses and of members long deceased is an invaluable tool. When I myself had charge of the roll I referred to it constantly: it gave me a mental picture both of the spread of our members and of family relationships; it posed questions to which I had to find answers and reminded me of people whom I had overlooked or neglected. It was with reluctance that I handed the book over to a new session clerk who wished, quite rightly, to have it for his own briefing of the district elders and oversight of the congregation. I have always, however, kept a pocket-size replica, with the names set out both alphabetically and in districts but without the recorded attendances at Communion. At each name I have noted the date, i.e. the year, of my last visit.

When was the Roll last purged? Purging is a delicate matter and no church of Jesus Christ should be ruthless about it. There are bound to be 'marginals' on it, people to whom we give the benefit of the doubt. But beyond the borderline cases there are those who, after many years of patient effort by ministers, elders and fellow-members, have shown not the slightest intention of returning to the fold. To keep their names—and in the course of a long ministry these may run into hundreds—on the Roll is to make it both misleading and valueless. They should be retained on a separate list, as those who, in the distant past, had taken vows of membership and been received; and a new minister may be the means of restoring them, when everyone else has failed. But to claim them as communicant members is unacceptable.

What are you yourself to do about those people who are seldom seen, and who are, as far as you can make out, non-practising members? They too are your flock and you are charged to care for them and for their spiritual welfare. Therefore the negative response that writes them off as dead wood and sees their removal as a refining of the congregation is not enough. They are a pastoral responsibility as well as a problem, and you may be the one to help them or, if not you, an elder, teacher or neighbour who shares your concern. The first task is to discover why they have ceased to function: and this has to be undertaken delicately. Only to those whom you know well, and whose friendship you have, can you say directly, 'Why don't you come to church?' With the majority it is a matter of probing gently; perhaps not even probing but getting to know the family and the circumstance and forming conclusions.

At the end of the day you will find that some respond to an attention and encouragement that they had never known before, and begin to identify themselves again with the Christian community. Others are grateful for your visits and promise to make a new start, but like the wheat in the parable soon wither away. Others again, who have only made use of the Church for a wedding or to secure some other benefit, will remain a problem.

Oversight of the Communicants' Roll is one of the Session's major responsibilities. Every year it is to be examined and brought up to date. To do this properly a whole evening, if not more, is required and there should be no other items on the agenda.

In such a delicate matter rule of thumb decisions are to be avoided. 'The rule,' some elder may insist, 'is that if anyone has not attended Communion during a period of three years, and there is no obvious reason such as infirmity or temporary absence from home, their name should be removed.' To enforce this, however, as if it were a law of the Medes and Persians would, as experienced ministers know, do untold harm. There are some who can, and should, be 'purged', and who will themselves accept the fact that their membership has ceased to mean anything at all. There are others who, even after three years, have not been sufficiently challenged or counselled: whose absence, whose attitude, or whose domestic difficulties, are unknown quantities. There are still others whose circumstances are not fully known by their district elder, but with whom the minister is involved and for whom he nurtures hope. To cut them off might be to abandon hope where some spark exists.

Fellowship

The way to create Christian fellowship is by cherishing the common life in Christ; by bringing people together to pray, to work, and to go out in mission and service together in Christ's name, to explore the Faith together and to share together in every aspect of the Christian task in their own place. It is, as someone has said 'not the contrived get-together of the soirée; it is the fellowship of the Spirit when people find themselves alongside each other in the common worship and service of Christ.'

You will, I know, accept all this. I am less certain that you will be with me when I say that contrived get-togethers, while not of the essence of the matter do, if handled properly, contribute to spiritual fellowship. For if friendships are widely fostered and cliques transcended those who worship and serve Christ together will do so as friends; and an extra dimension be added to their unity in Christ.

In other words, do not write off the social side. While not of the *esse* it may be of the *bene esse* of the Church. It may be there that we get to know one another. Afterwards when we come to Communion it means that some of those who serve and others beside us in the pews are 'kent faces'. They are an extension of our family; and surely to share in Communion with your own family is a special delight, beyond the joy of sharing in it with strangers.

Among all the possible activities there are two categories more in keeping with the essential nature of the Church than folk-dancing, yoga and weight-watching groups can ever be. First, the Pastoral Care Groups: those whose purpose is to cooperate with the minister in visiting and praying for those in pastoral need, the elderly and housebound, the sick (at home and in hospital), the bereaved, the deserted, the victims of misfortune and those not coping well; and those who meet for mutual encouragement like the Family Groups which have been described as 'an exciting area of the churches' evangel in our time'. In the latter a number of families meet together regularly with the aim of enriching one another through fellowship and extending that fellowship to other families.

Room should be made for those cells which are the seedbeds of new life; the Bible Study and Prayer Groups and the House Groups through which many congregations are renewed. Bringing together a wide age-range and creating an atmosphere whose friendliness induces frank and easy conversation, they also fulfil the therapeutic vocation of the Church.

A prime task of the minister is to create and promote such groups. He is in the best position to see who can lead them, as well as to know of those in congregation and parish who might respond to this kind of spiritual and social therapy. Through their creation he will, like Moses when he accepted the advice of Jethro, be sharing the pastoral burden.

The minister's own part in such groups can be invaluable, for he has much to give them. But with the best of intentions he sometimes fouls them up; either by undervaluing the lay contributions and being too quick to make his own, or by drawing every conversation round to his pet obsession—how to get people to come to church!

The other category which has a claim to priority is the group which combines fraternisation with some concern of the Christian conscience. From Amnesty International to Alcoholics Anonymous, and from peace and justice to ecology. It may be an action group concerned with community, race, or inter-church relations; or a healing group; a Third World group or a missionary fellowship. There is a wide range of such activities, and some unusual ones—for instance the liaison-group through which one Edinburgh congregation carries on joint activities with patients from a hospital for epileptics.

Many of these groups are small in numbers and struggling to exist because their concerns are, regrettably, caviar to the general. Yet is it not because of its apparent lack of concern for things that really matter that young people of conviction are often deterred from the Church and from the parish ministry?

As well as encouraging such activities, we should consider whether they might not be pursued more effectively on an ecumenical basis. The One World Group in the congregation of which I am now a member would, for instance, find it hard going but for the fact that it is supported by a Council of Churches and has members from four denominations. The 'Lund principle' that churches should only do apart the things they cannot do together is one which parish ministers should be quick to promote.

Our value-judgments, however, should not blind us to the propensities for fellowship inherent in some activities that are off-centre, such as a good dramatic club. Not only do people find a creative fulfilment in drama, and not only can it be used, more directly, in the service of religion; but the players are also drawn closely together in friendship.

As well as by the activities I have mentioned, fellowship is fostered by money-raising efforts. Some would dispute this, but it is so. Sales of Work periodically come under fire. It is said that they are sub-Christian, and that direct giving, expecting nothing in return, is the only Christian way. Also that they undercut the local tradesmen; and impose on those most deeply involved no little burden and strain. Or that they breed rivalries, competitiveness and greed—and a spate of dubious sideshows such as raffles, tombola, guessing games and bottle stalls depending on what is in the bottles.

All this is much exaggerated. The giving at church sales is for the most part all but 'direct'. For the Kirk, people will buy over and above what they need. The local tradesmen, far from feeling put upon, are quick to support them; often by contributing foodstuffs or prizes. And members who fail to give systematically to the Church often take the opportunity to make a special donation. Sure, there is some grumbling among exhausted workers that 'it was all left to the willing few'; but later on they are glad they did it, and volunteer again. Competitiveness and worldliness are familiar aberrations of human nature; but in the majority of church sales they appear on a very small scale and can be held in check.

The credit side far outweighs the other. Love and generosity towards the Church, work and sacrifice, fellowship in a common cause and, not least, a friendly spirit in which not only the church members but many others share, are all generated by such efforts. At a time when the sums raised by coffee mornings and sales are increasingly inadequate and fund-raising on a larger scale, and sometimes with professional help, is on the increase, there is still, on these grounds, a place for the Sale of Work.

But we must not fall into the error of supposing that the only real fellowship is one in which every member is engaged in the communal activities. There should be room for those who are not good mixers; who share in our love for Christ and His Church but would rather not be pressed into doing things which they find uncongenial; and who shrink from what to them, though not to most of us, are excessive expressions of friendship or intrusions into their privacy.

On the quiet ones then we must not impose more open-handed friendship than they can take, but let them be. And if they come regularly to worship and respond quietly to the appeals for support, whether it be by praying, or giving, or simply by being there when something significant is afoot, they may be doing more than many of

80

us who are more gregarious and outwardly busy. We need Mary as well as Martha. As for the stranger, he must find not just politeness, but warmth, which will not be a gushing bonhomie, for that is not our native style. Our office-bearers, especially, should be encouraged to greet the stranger (who in larger congregations is not easy to identify). But above all we should seek to create a worshipping community which is in the true sense evangelical; one which demonstrates the presence of a caring love, of such mutual openness and trust that those who come will know that they are in a fellowship, and in an atmosphere which is different, even unique, but not alien. Only in such a congregation can the communication of the gospel be effective. For it is the Holy Spirit, not ourselves, Who converts and, although He is not confined within the Church, Who there confirms the promise that when two or three are gathered together...

Because that gathering of our people together in Christ's name, which means in His fellowship and in His spirit, takes place also when Christians share in the fellowship of Iona and Taizé, of Keswick and Carberry, of Dunblane and Crieff, we should commend such centres of study and retreat. And, indeed, encourage our younger members to participate in youth conferences and assemblies, both near and far, and our older ones to venture into ecumenical circles; and some to visit Assisi, or the Kirchentag, or the Holy Land. All these are experiences which foster fellowship even while they open minds and spirits; they will also vitalize the local church community.

16 Fellow Workers

Pre-eminent among a Scottish minister's fellow workers are the members of the Kirk Session. Ordained to give leadership and to exert pastoral care, these men and women are also the policy-makers of the congregation and the potential power-house.

Not all the key people are on the Session. The Sunday School Superintendent, the President of the Guild, the Organist, the Scoutmaster, the Guide or Brigade Captain, the Cradle Roll Secretary, may or may not be there. They are equally to be esteemed as leaders.

But the relationship of minister and elders is a vital one. The oversight of the congregation and the ordering of its activities are in their hands: together they can either foster or hinder its life. Your elders are, to begin with, a package deal: you take what is given you. Even today there exist congregations where the belief persists that elders should be elderly, male, and chosen not primarily for their character and devotion but according to their position in the community. But the odds are on the package being a good one. There are few careerists in the Church, and most who accept office are dedicated Christians. And even the worst of Kirk Sessions, those whose outlook is narrow and intransigent and who lack vision and enthusiasm, contain individual members who are the salt of the earth. I would go further. By and large, it would be difficult to find a finer body of men and women anywhere than comprise the Scottish eldership.

If you are to value these fellow-workers you should take steps, as soon as possible, to know them individually. It will help if you ask them to take you once around their districts. (For 'foreign' readers: every elder in the Kirk has charge of a district and visits the members therein before each of the large statutory Communions, at the same time distributing the communion cards.) At heart you may prefer to find your own way, and enjoy discovering for yourself who is behind each door. You may also dislike the methodical, 'I will be visiting in District 1 this week' right on to 'I will be visiting in District 20'. Better to take people off guard, and not to disappoint them with a brief call when they had anticipated a lengthy one. However, the evenings spent with the elder and the chance for him to render this extra service and, in the bygoing, to talk over his district with you, outweigh the draw-

82

backs. And in the whole process the elder, as well as yourself, will learn much.

Another way of breaking the ice is to invite the elders and their spouses *en bloc* to the Manse. With a small Kirk Session my wife and I once did this on two successive evenings. After a buffet supper we gathered in one room, half of them sitting on the floor, and proceeded to chat, make music and play party games. Most of our guests had never been in the Manse before, nor had the Session ever met for a purely social occasion. These were eminently successful evenings and left their mark.

As Moderator (i.e. chairman) of the Kirk Session the minister is in a key position. From the chair he can exert leadership, contribute insights from the thinking of the wider Church, and share his vision of the way ahead. His leadership is not absolute. He should stand back and await the Session's verdicts as it makes its decisions. He should also look to the Session Clerk, especially in matters concerning the oversight of the elders, whose duties both at the Communion services and in their districts are in his hands. Large congregations may employ a separate rollkeeper, but normally the roll book, along with the Communion cards, is kept by the Session Clerk. It is the minister, however, to whom many people come wanting to join or disjoin; and who knows of a death, a marriage or a removal. And it is his duty to pass on regularly and speedily such information as the Clerk will require for the updating of the roll.

Before each meeting he should also consult the Clerk about the agenda, and ask whether he has received communications from the Presbytery or elsewhere.

One major obligation of the Kirk Session is to hold a watching brief over all the sectional activities. Left to themselves these are like an unpruned tree.

The major problem in most congregations is in finding leaders, and the elders should be asked, as they visit their districts, to take note of potential office-bearers, teachers, youth leaders, choir members, and so forth.

Those who already serve as leaders, from the Session Clerk and Treasurer to the Guiders and the regular distributors of magazines and flowers are, to a special extent, your fellow-workers. To be interested in what they are doing, sympathize with their frustrations and encourage them is a part of your calling. There is, perhaps, a cradle roll secretary, a missionary correspondent, a tea-convener, a Presbytery elder, a drama producer and someone who always organizes the Christmas decorations. And some without category who are known to you as special visitors to the housebound, the hospitals and those in various needs. These, and many more, are people to know, to appreciate, to support and pray for—as they will for you.

One with whom you will have many dealings is the church officer or beadle. He is not only 'the minister's man' but probably the hall-keeper as well, and his wife may be the church cleaner. Treat them with especial consideration for in a busy congregation they can be greatly harrassed. They may need your protection if inconsiderate organisations keep them from their bed by lingering on in the halls. If they are the custodians and have to prepare for successive groups and events on every day of the week, when do they get a night off? You may have to sort this out with the Property Convener or the Board. Or to see that the weekly day-off is recorded in their terms of employment and is adhered to. You should also see that the Board or its representatives are alert to any problems concerning the church officer's house.

Another key member is the Treasurer. In a large congregation his is very nearly a full-time occupation. Even in smaller ones I have known several who, after a few years' service, have asked to be relieved from its unremitting tasks. Although we cannot, as in many American churches, make it a full-time salaried post, we ought to do everything possible to lighten the load. To seek the appointment, for instance, of a Freewill Offering Treasurer with responsibility for the Covenant Scheme; or a small but active Finance Committee.

You yourself can support the Treasurer in a number of ways. First, you should bring home to the congregation the material needs of the whole Church and the obligations of its members. You must not do this carpingly nor with incessant talk of money; nothing so grates upon, and even offends, a congregation. But positively, showing the greatness of the work, and the lustre of a generous spirit. Very occasionally, coming down to earth, you might refer to the entirely unrealistic standard of giving that prevails in the contributions of many to their church.

Again, when the Treasurer issues an appeal in the magazine, an endorsement from the minister may reinforce it (but not always): the Treasurer may even be grateful for help in drafting his appeal, if he is conscious of lacking the literary touch.

You are also in a position to draw his attention to relevant Assembly and Presbytery reports and decisions on financial matters;

and you can procure literature for him, including the Annual Accounts of the National Church, from the Church Offices; and this is usually appreciated.

The voice of many a Treasurer is seldom heard, except in his own 'slot' at Board and Congregational meetings. It is easy, therefore, to take his work for granted. We should go out of our way to see that this does not happen by thanking him personally and paying the tribute due to him on all possible occasions.

The most important of all fellow-workers—dare I say it?—is the minister's wife (or in a few cases husband). She rightly protests that she married the man, not the job, and that she is not an unpaid assistant. It may be that if she fulfils well her task of looking after, supporting, and being the companion of her husband, that's it! But there is more to be said. In days gone by, the lady of the manse had a special niche in society and much was expected of her. In the congregation she had not only to set an example, but also to accept the burdens of leadership; and it went without saying that she was President of the Guild.

Egalitarianism, the emancipation of women, and working wives have put paid to that. Whether she pursues a career or not, she can now do as she pleases; take up church work or decline it, attend services and meetings or stay away, be a public or a private person. But in some parishes it is not so simple. In one bereft of leaders and where few have had the benefits of higher education, can a young wife, possibly a graduate and with a background of school and Guide leadership, withhold her help? I know of one sparsely scattered parish where, of necessity, she has not only to be the flower-lady, but the beadle and cleaner as well: she even rings the bell! There are many others where, as a matter of conscience, she takes on the teenagers, the young mums or the Brownies.

When she does any of these things, however, they should be done voluntarily and not because it is expected of her. No congregation has the right to command her services. Not even the Guild! This is now generally recognized and those who feel that speaking (and praying) in public is not their line and that they are not cut out for a teaching and leading role; as well as those whose daily work and home responsibilities drain their energies, are 'let be'.

17 Among the Children

Since children are an integral part of the Christian family, when that family meets for worship they should not be excluded. A children's hymn is one way of recognizing their presence, but not a sufficient one. After all, when it comes to hymns the child can participate in many that are not specifically for children in a way that he cannot in the adult sermon. I believe that nothing makes the children feel more at home in church than the 'word to the children', and that we should do our utmost to provide it.

But I question whether the areas of worship in which we engage before they leave for Sunday School—Invocation, Penitence and the Old Testament Lesson—are those most suitable for children. Might it not be better for them to go to Sunday School first and to join their families in the pews after the sermon? They would then share in the extrovert Intercessions and the closing acts of praise. To time their entry is not too difficult, and I have seen a service so ordered become marvellously alive with the entry of the children.

'Do you always have an object to show the children?' someone asked me. Often, yes, but *always* turns it into a gimmick—'What's he going to produce today?' And what is merely an aid becomes the chief concern. Nor does every subject require it. If I were giving a series of talks on Children in the Bible, or The Beatitudes of Jesus, or on the Scottish Saints I would not use them. Rather than show an Iona Cross in a talk on St Columba, I would show it *sui generis* in order to talk about its shape and meaning and perhaps to compare it with other crosses.

Another contact with younger children is the local Primary School. The headmaster may contact you; if not, you should invite yourself along. Most headmasters welcome the minister as the official 'Visitor' and come to a mutual agreement as to what you will do. Two lines, or a combination of them are possible. To take a School Assembly, probably weekly, or to go to the classrooms. I prefer the latter. To follow a syllabus with one age-group is more effective than speaking to infants and ten-year olds together. Fewer children will pass immediately through your hands, but everyone will eventually do so.

To which class should you offer your services? You may find that one has an especially sympathetic teacher, one of your own flock, who will support you in every way; whereas another has someone less responsive. You are tempted to choose the former; but, in fact, she is capable of giving good religious instruction herself, and does so—so I would take the latter.

The class having been put at your disposal, what are you to do with them? And how are you to do it? The task is a daunting one to those without a training in educational methods. The one thing to avoid is a prepared discourse. Teaching is not the filling of empty vessels. It is literally *educare*—to draw out, to make contact with the minds, however simple, of your pupils, to explore with them, and to share with them of your knowledge. If you have time to develop the use of audio-visual aids and teaching kits so much the better. If not, you may at least find that individual notebooks and the blackboard elicit a response.

In the selection of Sunday School teachers the potentialities of older people should not be overlooked. There is a tendency to go for youngsters fresh from the Communicants Class who are not yet office-bearers and have no other church employment. Up to a point this is good, not only for the children but for these young teachers who often find a stake in the church, and in its fellowship discover themselves. But the Sunday Schools need maturer teachers too, and some with a deeper understanding of children, born of experience. I recall two. A spinster, well over sixty whose knowledge of teaching methods was non-existent but whom her class of girls adored and from whom they learned, if nothing else, the love of Christ and the beauty of holiness. And a mother of four, teenagers and beyond, who controlled and taught a class of restive nine-year old boys with a loving authority which few fledgling teachers could match.

In days when active men and women are made redundant and early retirement leaves many with a vacuum in their lives, the possibility of a vocation as a Sunday School teacher should, at the very least, be brought to their notice. Older people are sometimes reluctant to undertake so responsible a work. Not so the very young. Girls in their early teens find easy solace for their burgeoning maternal instincts by helping in the Beginners Department; and for two pins they will leave the Bible Class to do so. Inasmuch as they need instruction more than the children need them, they should perhaps wait. Should the minimum age be seventeen?

18 Teenagers - Oh, Help!

Our Lord knew the teenager and his foibles. The boy who says 'Yes, Dad, I'll go and work in the vineyard'—or it may be the allotment or the garage—but who then forgets or is diverted. The girls who accept a responsible role at the wedding, but are feckless about filling their lamps; who think 'It will come right on the night' and when they find they have forgotten the oil expect to borrow it. And who, for all their good intentions, fall asleep on the job and miss the bridegroom—and the bus! And, of course, the prodigal, a lad who thought he could handle both money and life, and who rebelled against his home and family, but came an almighty cropper.

All teenagers are not like that; but you can recognize them there. You can also, I hope, recognise many in the boy who was sorry he had been churlish to his father, and did go and work in the vineyard; in the other bridesmaids who were conscientious and alert; and in the prodigal when he 'came to himself', a truer, less wayward self, and was ready to take his place in society. Youth leaders, along with their parents, are sometimes driven crazy by their coltish irresponsibility, and yet love them for the true selves with which they may or may not yet have come to terms. The leaders, with so much volatile material on their hands need a good deal of backing in their work: and this we can give.

In your own dealings with the young, the essential thing is to take them seriously; and neither to talk down nor patronise. And while identifying with their feelings and sharing in their interests, not to pretend to be anything other than what you are. As a character in a novel reflects, 'It was no use speaking to the young as if you were young yourself. If you did, they distrusted you' (C.P. Snow, *Last Things*, p. 240). They neither expect nor want you to talk their lingo or exhibit their mannerisms. To swagger, to be boisterous and irreverent, and puppy-like with restless energy and mischief; all this comes naturally to them, but not to you if you are even ten years older than they are. In a gap of twenty years the gaffe is so much the greater.

We were just beginning to unpack at the manse when a youth tore up the drive on his bike, scattering the gravel as he braked. He wore a busman's cap on the back of his head and appeared a likely lad.

'Hallo' said I. 'Hallo' said he, 'are you going to start a youth club?' This early confrontation, I knew, was crucial. If I hemmed and hawed he and his mates would write me off. But if I showed willing and there was no one else to lead it... ? 'It might be a good idea,' I said, 'but what's the form? What is there for young people?' 'Nothing'. 'Then what do you do with yourselves?' 'Just hang around'. 'And if you had this youth club, are there enough of you to keep it going? And would you be prepared to act as leaders, secretary, treasurer, committee members and so on?' 'Sure.' 'But you couldn't just elect yourselves, you'd have to wait and see what everyone wanted: and where would you meet, and what would you do?' With a mixture of caution and encouragement I imparted to him that I would at any rate follow up the proposal. And a month or two later the Community Association, newly formed, considered the matter. They already knew the need, and two couples (younger-middle aged) actually volunteered to get a club going. It soon became part of the landscape and though it fluctuated as most do, it has continued to supply a need.

Two things ensured its success. It had a combined senior-junior leadership, with the adults exercising necessary control but listening to the juniors, and the members saying what they wanted and often getting it; and, secondly, it was a community venture which had widespread support in the village. Had it been established and run by the church it would have had a narrower membership and less backing. I may be wrong: but though I had qualms about its dissociation from the church, these were offset by the quality of the initial and subsequent leadership. The first leaders were kirk elders and their wives: no coincidence, for many volunteers for community service are church folk. They were the best kind of church folk in that they neither wore labels nor proselytised. Their friendship and their own life-style provided a Christian presence; and their welcoming attitude to myself as the parish minister meant that I had opportunities to meet the club members; to attend their concerts, their A.G.M., their Old Folks Supper, their games awards, and so on; and to invite them to join in Christian Aid activities and some special occasions at the church.

Most ministers would prefer a Youth Fellowship to a Club. For in the former there is discussion and worship. To insist on these in a Club may be disastrous. In a church-sponsored club, it is possible to say 'At 10 o'clock there will be an Epilogue'—better still, have it at 9 as an Interlude, and they will not start leaving! It is also possible to appoint church people (e.g. members of the Kirk Session) to visit them. But when the membership is not oriented towards the church one has to tread warily. (In the community club described above I suggested to the Committee that they might care to have a series of short discussion-points; but when they put this to the members it was vetoed.)

You may go to a church which already has a Youth Fellowship. Visit it, but give them their head. Sit in often, but speak little.

Where there is no Youth Fellowship I do not say that you should immediately start one. What else is there? Possibly some other study or action group, or a house-church where their presence would be of more use to other people, and more beneficial to themselves.

The Churches are now looking again at the three traditional models of Bible Class, Open Youth Club, and Youth Fellowship, and finding some alternatives: cell groups, Justice and Peace groups, and various *ad hoc* groups engaged in projects, in study or in spiritual exploration. And for rural areas travelling groups are suggested—where no one church can sustain its own youth work, but the churches together in an area can sponsor a group which meets on the different premises in turn.

The young people who belong to the uniformed organizations are more conformist. They will welcome the minister, who is probably their chaplain, as often as he cares to come, and will not only respond to his invitations to church parades or youth services but also expect him to provide acts of worship at their camps as well as *in situ*. Where we can be of most help to these organizations, and in fact to every kind of youth group, is in their chronic search for leaders. From Sunday School to Brownies the cry is never 'Too many Chiefs, too few Indians' but the reverse. (Well, not entirely, for the Indians often have other hunting-grounds.) But as a talent-spotter the minister can be invaluable. To quote an instance which gave me considerable satisfaction. When a Boys Brigade Company lost their Captain and no Lieutenant was able to replace him, I was able to 'sell' them someone who had had no B.B. experience but was a former Scoutmaster and during the War had risen through the ranks to become a commissioned officer. They took to him, and he to the Brigade like the proverbial duck, and he made a great success of it.

And what of the Minister's Bible Class? As an assistant it was my first assignment. I recalled the Bible Classes of my youth. There the minister had lectured us on great Christian books, introducing us to Bunyan, Wesley, Penn, Herbert *et al*.

So I tried to go one better, introducing more recent books. I recall Constance Padwick's *Temple Gairdner* and Studdert Kennedy's poems. And I found, and over twenty years later found again, that while the spiritual and literary writings are too rarified for that age-group, down-to-earth biography always appeals—whether it be Livingstone or Schweitzer, Gladys Aylward, Eric Liddell or the characters in *Miracle on the River Kwai*. More recently, surely, such as Geoff Shaw, Jean Waddell, Mother Teresa, and the Christian leaders and 'dissidents' in South Africa, Russia and South America.

Amid all the contemporary material, whether presented through a kit or in leaders' handbooks, the opportunity should not be missed of introducing saints and heroes of today, as well as those of the past.

The snag, of course, is that unless one has time to put together some kind of visual and dramatic presentation, or the materials on which to do group research, one falls back on the lecture method. And that is surely inappropriate in a small group. My own policy would be to work out a syllabus in which the straight talk is only introduced at reasonable intervals, and in which there are abundant opportunities for the members to participate. They need instruction more than senior groups such as Youth Fellowships do. But if the topic be, for example, the centrality, or essentiality, of the Bible it can be approached by asking 'In what sense is the Bible true?' and eliciting ideas and opinions.

It is sad to see a minister who is unaware of his limitations fail with his Bible Class while a capable lawyer, education officer or civil servant stands by unused; or to see a minister who has much to give stand aside while the class is relegated to a layman accepted for his zeal, but perhaps narrow or old-fashioned in outlook.

Worship should never be forgotten. Unless the Bible Class members are also attending services—and this can never be assumed—their only experience of it will be in the class. And to help them to worship is part of the leader's task. In a small group it should be informal and resemble the atmosphere of family prayers rather than of a church service. Liturgical formulae such as 'Let us hear the Word of God' are unsuitable, though the simple rituals of standing to pray, reading prayers in unison and saying responses may be so. To encourage the group to take part also brings reality. Singing may be impractical through lack of numbers but the hymnbook can be explored with the aid of musical instruments, tapes and cassettes.

Much as we desire for our young people that they should know Christ early and be committed to Him in church membership, we should be aware of the danger of plucking unripe fruit or, as someone said, 'of subjecting adolescents to a kind of spiritual sheep-dip, which becomes no more than a brief interlude of priggishness and religiosity in a lifetime of indifference.' The truth is that some will be ready for confirmation even before they leave the class; others not until they have developed further in Youth Fellowship or in their maturing. So, although I would publicise the Communicants' Class I would not press it on them; but privately there might be one or two whom I would approach and say 'You may be interested. Don't come because I say so, but you'll be welcome if you do.'

Eagerness to be involved in some sphere of the Church's work, however, in preference to passive instruction in a class indicates a fundamental need. 'Adolescence is a time for the espousal of causes.' Young people need to be involved and to serve. The senior Sunday School or older youth group which will hold them is the one which is pursuing a project, whether it be sponsoring a guide dog, raising money for a wheel chair, 'adopting' someone in need, cleaning and decorating old people's houses or digging their gardens.

19 The Parish Pump, and Beyond

A noteworthy advance in the life of the Church is that congregations have become more outgoing, especially in their involvement in social care. The command to feed the hungry, heal the sick and succour the poor and the distressed has always been recognized as part of the Church's mission; but now it occupies a more central place. As has been said, formerly we went out to serve our fellow-men because Christ had commanded us to do so; now we go out because we have seen that He is in our needy neighbour. We must meet up with Him and work with Him there.

The needs to which the Church reaches out are not only material, physical and social, but also spiritual. The parish church's concern is that all who live in the parish and as many as we can reach beyond it should know the love of God, expressed in many practical ways, and share in the unsearchable riches of Christ.

This is why we not only go out to people but want to bring them in; not, as is alleged, to swell our numbers but to share the spiritual resources of the Church. When we see a cross-section of the community on its knees, praising God and confessing that Jesus is Lord, we naturally want people to come to church. We are unhappy when they take churchgoing lightly, arguing that you can stay away and be as good a Christian anyhow. So we make strenuous efforts to recapture the lost churchgoers, and fish, as our Lord told us to, for new disciples. Part of our outreach is obviously evangelism—or, if you prefer it, mission.

For the minister outreach is inevitable, for he is concerned for everyone in his parish. A point well made by my own minister within whose parish bounds Edinburgh's Waverley Station stands. On learning that a new manager had been appointed to the Station Hotel, he at once wrote to welcome him and say, 'We are your parish church and if at any time we can be of service...'

Similarly, should your parish contain any other community within the community, social, commercial, educational, industrial or sporting, there is a potential role for the parish minister, that of 'honorary padre'. It should also go without saying that friendship towards other religious bodies, including those of other faiths, and towards every individual in the community should be our hallmark, and that we should go out of our way to greet incomers, tourists and visitors.

A parish visitation or a mission of friendship held not once in a generation, but at intervals of perhaps five or six years seems the least that we can do.

To inaugurate a parish visitation, you will have to devise a tentative programme and lay it before the Kirk Session. And there you may, I repeat may, encounter objections and buckets of cold water! Who is going to do it? What will it cost? When can it be fitted in? What kind of results do you expect? Is it not a waste of time? Do we want people coming to our organizations who are not really interested in the Church? Have we not plenty to do chasing up our own members?

You should make it plain that while you seek the Session's support, you are not expecting them to shoulder the entire burden. It is the congregation's pigeon, as well as theirs: and you will be looking for volunteers from every quarter.

Having set your hand to the plough, you will have it there for a considerable time; and your leadership will be required at every stage. As in warfare the effective officers lead from in front, and share both the dangers and the discomforts, so you will take your part. That part, however, will be a more specialized one. Perhaps you will wait until the visitors return, and having consulted with them, go to where it would seem that a call from the minister is the best follow-up.

At such a time of special outreach the Session might consider whether a teaching and preaching mission should not run concurrently. This will multiply the work but it should not devolve wholly on yourself. On one such campaign, we not only imported another minister, an outstanding communicator, for a series of meetings which climaxed on the second Sunday evening; we also had members of the congregation—e.g. a housewife, a B.B. officer, a young mother, and the Session Clerk, giving five-minute talks on 'What the Church means to Me'. As the week progressed the attendances grew, and not a few strangers returned afterwards. Admittedly this was some years ago. These methods might be less effective today. The discos, films and lively socials which featured then, however, would still play their part.

The method you employ will depend on the resources at your disposal. If you cannot raise the numbers for a full-scale effort, why not a mini-mission to a section of your parish? Take four city streets, for instance. A handful of visitors could cover these in a week; but

94

more effectively in a fortnight. I know of one city church which tackles a third of its parish each year. In Edinburgh the ideal time is immediately after the autumn holiday—i.e. starting on the third Tuesday of September. A ten-day visitation then would conclude just as the various congregational activities began their winter session.

As Ezekiel 'sat where they sat' among the exiles in Babylon and as St Paul made himself 'all things to all men'; above all, as Jesus mixed freely with all types and conditions, so must we.

A spirit of openness and a knowledge of the cultural context of our own country and neighbourhood, are prerequisites of evangelism. Nor can it consist of sporadic forays led by a Billy Graham, a Louis Palau, or anyone else. Whatever methods are employed they should be those that best suit the native temperament and scene. But more essential than techniques is the permanent spirit and motivation of the congregation. One of our perennial tasks as ministers is, under God, to create and foster an evangelical people, a people to whom neighbourliness within the congregation is not enough, but who reach out in concern for the community and the world.

We may, of course, ignore the other denominations or preserve an amicable coexistence. But that will neither heal the wounds of Christendom, nor enable us to work and witness in any but a limited way. We may come together, or exchange pulpits, on such designated occasions as the Week of Prayer for Unity. But although at one time that was a move forward, it has become a familiar gesture which achieves little.

What then? We must continually explore ways and means of closer contact and grass-roots ecumenism, and have such a relationship that we can learn from one another and worship, study and make common cause.

Social witness and social action are responsibilities not only of the Church but of every local congregation. To remind people that the world is at their doorstep and the Third World their concern is part of the minister's task; and to urge them to be politically committed (without, of course, preaching party politics) and to earth their Christian profession in the soil of the real world.

Because they are partners in the world-wide Church our members should be aware of their fellow-Christians in other lands, especially non-Christian lands: they should be praying for them, learning from them and working with them.

One of the best ways of doing this is through each parish church adopting a missionary partner; and this is widely done. The partner, a minister working with the Central African Presbyterian Church or the Church of North India; a social worker in Jamaica, an accountant in Zambia, a theological teacher in Taiwan, an agriculturalist in Bangladesh, nurses and community workers in many fields—is a window through which we can see, as in no other way, what goes on. The parish minister does not himself have to be the missionary's link-man. The Church of Scotland in its Partner Plan asks each congregation to appoint someone who will both receive and distribute the missionary's quarterly letters and correspond with him. The minister's part is to see that this is being done, to welcome the missionary on his homecoming and invite him to the pulpit and/or to meet with the congregation in any of its groupings. The minister should also remember to pray in church, on such occasions perhaps, as the quarterly Communion, World Mission Sunday and St Andrewstide, for the missionary partner by name.

Part V
AND FURTHERMORE

20 Also on the Agenda

Groups

Any success I had with groups was sporadic and ephemeral. But I regard this as a shortcoming, and acknowledge that whenever such a group has been formed (usually in preparation for a parish mission or a World Assembly, or at a Guild's, or similar organization's, annual Bible Study Night) minds and hearts have become alive, relationships been deepened and the fellowship of the Holy Spirit, the *koinonia*, has become real.

One difficulty is that the minister, academically trained, often fails to distinguish between study and exposition. Or, if he is an intellectual, he may queer the pitch of those in the group whose approach is primarily that of the heart and of spiritual understanding, who are apt to sing dumb in the presence of textual expertise; then tire of a passive role and fall away.

It also has to be said that some ministers deprecate and discourage Bible study groups. Letting ordinary folk loose on the Bible, they say, is a waste of time; for either they will contribute something vague and woolly and miss the point, or they will find a superfluity of points and look for introspective meanings. Far better that we should simply expound the Bible from the pulpit.

We should neither be obtrusive nor too anxious to lead and direct the thinking of our study groups, but leave room for the Holy Spirit to open up the truth. Nor must we assume that as leader the minister is the automatic choice. On the contrary, almost an endemic failing among ministers is their inability to lead group discussions. An inter-church group was stumped once for a speaker to complete its syllabus. The assignment was a brief talk, evoking a ten-minutes discussion. 'Why not your own minister?' I asked the secretary: 'he's lively, his preaching is good and so are his broadcasts.' 'To tell the truth,' she replied, 'his wife would make a far better job of it. The trouble with him is he never knows when to stop—he's no good in a group; he always dominates it.'

When the leader is prepared to hold back, and not only to await but gently to extricate the views of others, he is rewarded. How easy it is, for example, having selected a simple, familiar topic such as the Prodigal Son, for a Guild or young mothers' discussion evening, to find out who would want to belt the young delinquent or who would throw a party! Was the father too soft, and was the elder brother too hard? When someone has gone astray, should they be allowed to forget it? The simple questions that arise concerning conduct and human relationships should not only loosen tongues, but in due course, as Jesus intended, raise deeper thoughts about God. But to begin at the other end, as I regret to say many ministers would do, with a homily on what Jesus meant by it all, and then to say 'Have you any questions?' is to kill it stone dead.

I shall not describe the various methods of Bible study. There is ample literature on the subject. But I would like to mention one of which I am fond; that Swedish method which consists of each member sketching a candle, a question-mark and a sword, and under each of them jotting his thoughts. Under the *candle*, any illuminations or insights the passage has brought. Under the *question-mark*, any questions it has posed regarding theology or life, any difficulties in the text, or any doubt about its relationship to other Bible teaching. Under the *sword*, any way in which the whole or a part has pierced the conscience or entered the heart. When the findings of the group are compared this exercise, as well as being revealing, leads on to deeper discussion.

Christian Aid

Another 'extra' is Christian Aid. Those who have seen at first hand the sufferings and poverty of the Third World cannot fail to observe, when they return home, the Church's preoccupation with its own worship and internal discipline rather than an openness to world need. Although it takes time and effort, therefore, we should do all in our power to support Christian Aid. Among the other humanitarian organizations whose concern is world poverty—Oxfam, War on Want, Unicef, etc., Christian Aid is peculiarly the arm of the Churches. The aid is given without discrimination of race or religion, but it is collected by the Churches from the communities around their doors, and at the receiving end indigenous Churches are involved in its fair distribution.

The information which Christian Aid broadcasts by films, posters and up-to-date literature is both challenging and educative; alerting us to the inequalities and tragedies of the world we live in, and informing us of a thousand imaginative projects through which charitable hand-outs become more than temporary alleviants and are creative for the future. The congregations which are given opportunity to participate in this are fortunate, and their own spiritual growth is enhanced.

If then you find yourself in a charge which has taken no part in Christian Aid, what are you to do? I suggest that you put it to the Kirk Session that, out of deep conviction, you are seeking their support for the formation of a Christian Aid Committee. There may be fears that this will mean (a) further fund-raising in a congregation already heavily burdened; and (b) asking the busiest church-workers to be busier still. To allay such fears you should emphasise (a) that the fund-raising is *through* rather than *in* the congregation. Giving is voluntary and if the Committee should, in their enthusiasm, wish to organize any special efforts these will not be a charge on the congregation; and (b) that the Committee need not be confined to the usual workers and certainly not to the office bearers. Indeed, though initiated by the Session, it might well be a community committee. In my own parish it included the laird's wife who is a Roman Catholic, the Football Club Secretary and the President of the Community Youth Club: and at a later stage it was the non-church Girls Club and Young Wives who undertook the door-to-door collection. Where no group will do the door-to-door double stint, it may be possible to enlist individuals to collect from their own street.

Having secured the support, ardent or lukewarm, of the Kirk Session and taken the initiative in setting up a Committee, what next? Make the link with the nearest Christian Aid Office, which will supply any amount of information and suggestions. Then devolve the work onto the committee members and anyone else whom they wish to co-opt. Among others we co-opted the Primary Headmaster who held a Christian Aid Poster Competition at the school, and the School Cook who had the wherewithal to provide soup for those who went on the Sponsored Walk.

Your particular assignment is to initiate the Week with an appropriate church service, and a sermon which both informs and gives the Christian motivation; to take part yourself in the fund-raising events; and both to give encouragement throughout and to remember to thank those who have contributed in various ways.

Finally, on Christian Aid Sunday you may be able to do more than focus the worship on Christ's love for the poor. You can, perhaps, summon your people to express that love in some visible act. That which most readily comes to mind is a Soup and Cheese Lunch in the church hall. But here are two variants in which I have taken part. The eight English-speaking congregations in Rome have 'Operation Rice Bowl' with its slogan 'Skip or skimp a meal and give a donation instead to the hungry in [say] Ethiopia.' Papier mâché bowls are made by the children, distributed among the congregations, and dedicated at the appropriate services. The other variant, in Edinburgh, was a Lunch at which, for £1 a head, the congregation and their friends sat down to a bowl of rice and lentils, while four of their number, drawn by lot, sat embarrassingly in the middle and tucked in to a normal lunch, supplied free with all appurtenances, including wine, by the 5-star hotel next door. The message did not have to be spelled out, and £100 went to Christian Aid.

The parish magazine

The parish magazine should be seen by those who produce it as a medium through which to communicate the Gospel. I do not mean that it should become a tract, couched in religious language and with a direct come-to-Jesus appeal. Such an approach defeats its own ends, and successive issues before long make a quick exit to the wastepaper basket.

I mean rather that we should try to get the ear of the unbelievers and half-believers who are likely to come across it; and by the way we discuss public issues and perennial problems of human relationships and morality, convince them that Christianity has relevance. By the way we write of the Church and its Lord, by the concern we show in His name for 'all sorts and conditions' in the community, we will reveal that for us He is alive and that the congregation up the road is a welcoming one, and reflects His mind and spirit. Our overriding aim should be to do this and, in doing so, to produce a magazine more pointed and less innocuous than most; one whose lay-out attracts, and where a forum is to be found for the tremendous issues, both spiritual and ethical, with which thoughtful churchmen and many people beyond our walls are concerned.

The Bookstall

To find someone to run a bookstall is not too difficult. But you will probably have to select the books yourself, and perhaps choose a Book of the Month and promote it in the magazine. As a retired minister this is a job I have been able to do for the congregation to which I belong, and other retired people with some knowledge of religious publications might be willing conscripts. Not many working laymen are free to go and browse in church bookrooms, where the selection of a stall may take an hour.

The bookstall is not a commercial venture. If it were, it would feature heart-warming stories and picture-books for the children; and have a minimal theological and devotional content. There may well be a sprinkling of the former, but the overall purpose is to help people to advance in their religious understanding and to learn more of what God is doing and has done in the world, through individual lives and through the Churches. There should be books to confirm beliefs already held, and not from any one theological viewpoint, but mind-stretching, and catholic in range, and others which discuss the religious doubts and moral dilemmas of today. Whether you include anything of theological weight will depend on your clientele: in a congregation which has members of the professions, graduates, students and people accustomed to sustained reading I would certainly do so.

The Church Library

Allied to the bookstall is the church library. A neglected, out-of-date library, like tattered hymnaries and shagged bibles in the pews does nothing for the congregation's image. But a carefully-selected one, added to annually by grants and donations is an asset, especially to those not in touch with bookshops or who cannot afford to buy. Where there is a large Sunday School staff a separate teachers' library should also be considered, and the minister can help by feeding information to the teachers as to how to set about it and what grants are available.

Committees

Take your part and, as you are able, play a constructive role in both the Courts and Committees of the Church. The minister who told me he was on thirty committees could scarcely do that; he would have insufficient time to ponder the issues. Besides, he was doing himself, his parishioners and his fellow-ministers no good; some of the latter were denied the chance of making their contribution.

Why do some people do this; accept an absurd number of appointments? They may not intend to, but one thing leads to another and they have never said no. Or they may suffer—as no servant of the Gospel should—from self-importance, careerism and the love of power. I should add that many whose motives are impeccable find themselves landed with overmuch Presbytery and Assembly work. You become a Presbytery Convener and are automatically appointed to the corresponding Assembly committee. There you are put on two sub-committees, and become a representative on various joint-committees; and so it goes on. You may even end up commuting to London for meetings of the British Council of Churches or its working-parties. And, further afield, in the service of a Confessional group or the W.C.C., and in preparation and follow-up meetings for their Consultations and Assemblies.

This over-involvement affects comparatively few; and some with an exceptional gift for it may have such a vocation. But for most of us the wise course is to accept only a few extra-parochial assignments and to be conscientious in pursuing them.

At the plenary meetings of Presbytery and Assembly you should certainly contribute when you have something to say. I am never happy when someone, in a retirement speech, says self-approvingly 'This is the first time I have raised my voice in Presbytery'. Down the years there was surely some occasion on which he should have been heard. I am still less happy to observe some newcomer establishing a dubious reputation by forever leaping to his feet. The best contributions are made by those who speak from knowledge and experience and have weighed up what they wish to say. And never, no never, begin with 'You will be glad to know that I shall be brief'. It is not a lie, for you believe it; but, as everyone else expects, it is probably a wild inaccuracy.

Extras
I have said nothing of those extras which take the form of unlooked-for problems. Every householder knows that one day the plumber will have to be sent for, a domestic crisis blow up, or finances require immediate attention. It happens in the church. Dry rot is found in the roof, the organ or the heating system fails, the Treasurer resigns or some scandal breaks out. Such events are disruptive of time and energy, but in overcoming them personal ties are strengthened, and the

congregation, surmounting each crisis, goes forward with confidence renewed.

Pilfering

An unlooked for problem we could well do without is pilfering. When it is from the church there is little you can do about it, apart from keeping more constant watch or, being unable to employ a custodian, having regrettably to lock the doors. Pilfering from the plate is a rare occurrence. It happened twice in my ministry and the Kirk Session wisely hushed it up.

21 Vocational Hazards

Most of our actions, like the city set on a hill, cannot be hid. This is why in our Presbyterian ordination vows we are asked to be 'godly and *circumspect*', an archaic word which means 'taking everything into account'. Being so much in the public eye we have to be not only on our best behaviour but singularly discreet.

To set out self-consciously to avoid all possible criticism however, is a form of paranoia. There is no need to slink into a cinema or slip away furtively to the golf course for fear that you will be accused of slacking. You either are a slacker or you are not, and the truth will out. We should not worry overmuch about what people think of us; nor complain about the liabilities of being in the limelight. As with politicians and sportsmen, royalty and 'show-biz' people, this just goes with the job. Exposed and vulnerable, we must learn to live with criticism. And when we drop a clanger we can only bite our tongues and hope to live it down.

Early on I learned a lesson about discretion. The occasion was the appointment of a new Church Officer. The Session were discussing the candidates, among whom was Mr F. He was a diligent, honest man, but of a rather hard-bitten appearance, and his words were few and blunt. 'He's a nice chap' I remarked, 'but isn't he rather a rough diamond?' A few days later I happened to call on his wife, a faithful if formidable member. She regarded me with a baleful eye and said accusingly, 'What did you say about my husband at the Kirk Session?' Someone else had been indiscreet! I could only apologise and explain that I would call Simon Peter, too, a bit of a rough diamond, and that no insult was intended; but it was a year or two before she appeared mollified. So, like Agag, we have to walk delicately. Year in, year out this is not easy. I have empathy with the minister who, on being asked, 'What are you most looking forward to in retirement?' replied 'Not having to be too careful about offending people.'

Criticism
The carping of critics will also reach your ears. The human capacity for denigration, especially in a closed society, is a fearsome thing. The age-old proverbs of the prophet without honour, and familiarity

breeding contempt bear that out. Some folk are never pleased. Either the minister is not visiting, or he visits this one and not that one. Either he neglects his garden, or he spends too much time in it. Either he made some awful remark from the pulpit or he neglected to support some pressure group. Either he failed to recognise someone, or he snubbed them. He may even have overlooked an engagement, or not been around when he was expected to be there—black marks indeed. And there are so many minor pitfalls like forgetting an intimation or promising 'I'll see to that' and failing to do so.

Even when there are good grounds for criticism, when it is hostile or rude it hurts; which may be what your assailant intended. What can you do? There is no room in the ministry for self-pity or taking the huff. You can only accept it, forget it, and carry on, making your peace, if need be, with God and, as far as in you lies, with your detractors.

Discouragement

A similar hazard, which you must learn to ride, is discouragement. The more ardent you are the more you will meet with it. You may find that there is little backing for some of your schemes; that few keep pace with you; and that your dreams for the congregation far from being shared are not even understood.

We can be dispirited too by self-doubt. 'What am I doing? Am I just wasting my own and other people's time? Where are the results?' But these are useless queries; and lacking in faith. Compare the disciples' question when Mary of Bethany poured the spikenard; 'To what purpose is this waste?' To Jesus it was no waste, but an offering of love. And so are our seemingly wasted efforts if they are given as to Him. Results—well, these are sometimes evident, more often not, and seldom immediately. We sow seeds and their fruition may take years. Faith alone is the answer to self-doubt.

You can doubt the ministry itself. You may feel that you are only on the periphery of modern life; that there is little resemblance, or even relevance, between the ways in which your days are spent and the more cohesive employment of others. I am sure that these misgivings afflict sector ministries even more than ours. A chaplain in the army or in industry is the odd man out; in a great organization geared to warfare and defence, or to mass-production, he is, in a sense, but an onlooker. It is only by clinging to his belief in the value of someone being there who is commissioned by Christ and His Church, and through the gradual process of getting to know people, that he will overcome the sense of futility: a process made easier in the parish by the more obvious desire for his services. Then one of the joys of the ministry is that it is full of the unexpected, and of serious and moving and humourous events. As when, for example, a young elder appeared at Vestry Hour to tell me he felt a call to the ministry.

Harrassment

There are also the inevitable hazards of being 'a man for others'. People of inadequate personality may plague and pester us. We should deal graciously with them for they are also God's children. Do not choke them off, but when they become a nuisance explain gently that you have somewhere to go, someone to see or work to attend to.

The unmarried minister is particularly vulnerable. The young minister should be careful not to give unwitting encouragement. Even when genuinely fond of someone in his congregation he should show the utmost restraint. If it turns out that there is indeed a relationship with a possibility of marriage, even there prudence demands a singular discretion.

Family problems

The minister's wife and family share in the difficulties imposed by his vocation. His wife's dilemma has been well described by Eric James: 'She shares to some extent the separation of the priest. Her friendships in the parish will be less easy... She will have to bear the fact that her husband belongs in a special sense to everyone else as well as to herself; and whilst he is a priest to the rest of the people, the fact that she is his wife will make it much more difficult for him to be a priest to her' (*Odd Man Out?*, Hodder & Stoughton, 1962, p. 62).

The fact that during his children's schooling he is liable to move once, or even twice, is profoundly disturbing to his family. The children, uprooted, will have to adjust to new schools and make new friends. They may already be under some stress through being regarded as the manse children. Instead of being accepted for what they are they are assigned a role. It may be ill-defined but it is there; and they too are 'odd men out'.

To some natures this will be a thorn in the flesh. I know of one daughter of the manse who when she moved out of church circles and went to college said, 'Thank God, I can be myself at last!' Others, in rebellion against being cast in a priggish or puritanical role, have been known to kick over the traces. One (not my own) was so incensed at being singled out and introduced as the minister's daughter that she eventually erupted with 'Cut the bloody credits'!

Beggars

Should you observe a chalk mark near your front door it may be one beggar telling another beggar where to find bread: 'bread' neither in the spiritual nor even the literal sense but in its slang connotation. The hazard of beggars at the manse, and also at the church, though less insistent in recent years, is still there, especially in the cities, and to those ministers known on their grapevine to be a soft touch.

The problem in listening to their hard-luck stories is to tell the false from the true, and the inexperienced minister is easily taken in. You will be told that because it is Friday evening the Social Security Office is closed until Monday; or that they have to obtain lodgings and an address to qualify for assistance and meanwhile face a week's starvation; or that all they need is their fare to Newcastle or Carlisle where a mate has a job lined up; or, more modestly, they may only ask for something for a meal and a bed.

What are you to do? Even before the doorbell rings you should have enquired of your fellow-ministers whether the Presbytery or Fraternal has any policy on the matter and what your clerical neighbours do. At the very least some will warn you to beware of a chap with cross-eyes called Jimmy whose wife is alleged to have left him! You should also seek advice of a more professional nature. At one stage I was helped by having an employment officer in the Kirk Session: it could be an aftercare officer, a social worker, someone working in Social Security or in the Police.

One thing the experts will tell you is that when people say they cannot get help they are probably bogus. For there is provision for the penniless and the homeless, and you will be counselled to harden your heart and turn them away. As a minister of the Gospel you may feel that this is over-harsh. What if this case, be it only one in a hundred, is genuine? It may be someone who has fallen through the social net; or who, through ignorance, has failed to put his case properly and not received his due. Had I any option, for instance, when a van full of children turned in at the manse drive on a Sunday evening? The parents, heading for Newcastle, had, they said, miscalculated on petrol and money, and the tank was almost empty. They signed an I.O.U. but it was never redeemed.

At the best, we can only give temporary relief in the hope that the next day, or after the weekend, something better may crop up. The material handout, however, even where we think it justified, should be given with a certain scepticism and in the form of a chit to the grocer or to a lodging-house rather than in cash. While the genuine down-and-out will accept these gratefully, disgust will appear on the sponger's face, for that is not what he was looking for; 'the price of a bed' really meant the price of a pint or two.

Perils of professionalism

A serious hazard is that of becoming ministerial. Almost without being aware of it we can adopt an off-putting professional manner. Not by being primly pious or hopelessly unworldly and shockable; nor by sounding unctuous. These characteristics, relished by lampoonists, have well-nigh gone. But by becoming less human in more subtle ways; a little pompous and pedantic perhaps.

Pomposity may take the form of referring in a proprietary way to 'my Kirk Session', 'my Guild', 'my organist', even 'my church'. Anyone else would almost certainly speak collectively and refer to 'our church', 'our choir', 'our Sunday School'. We, no less than they, belong to the fellowship, and would do well to emulate those African Christians who have only collective words in their vocabulary. Otherwise we sound possessive and egotistic.

We would also do well to stress 'we' rather than 'you' in our preaching. Otherwise we distance ourselves from other people. It is 'them' and 'us'. This may contribute to the erection of a barrier between the Church and those outside it; a barrier which is also raised when we speak an in-language and revolve in a churchy world which to the secular-minded appears an enclosed and esoteric society.

Too many of our compatriots feel that we churchmen disapprove their way of life, and that we talk another language; a situation we can only remedy by avoiding all pomposity, religiosity and churchianity and staying thoroughly human.

Even in the first decade of a busy ministry one can feel that there is too much of everything; and fall into the routine visit, the habitual prayers, the same tired old phrases. The sacraments can become a routine when you have dispensed them a hundred times. The 'Occasional Offices'—weddings and funerals, so called in the sense of 'used only as occasion demands', are far from occasional and easily dulled by custom.

One is tempted therefore, when stale or hard pressed to go to a marriage or funeral unprepared and regurgitate the service in its most familiar form. By the grace of God it is possible to do this and make it more than a routine, just as we can recite the well-worn phrases of the Lord's Prayer and the Apostles' Creed and inject such faith and feeling into them that they speak to us and to those with us afresh. Yet the hazard remains, and can only be disposed of by interspersing one's busyness with times of deliberate withdrawal and spiritual renewal.

Part VI
A CHARGE TO KEEP

22 Taking the Strain

As a minister you will never have the luxury of being able to spend all your time the way you want to. You seem to be at everyone's beck and call. To make too much of this, however, is to forget that it is a dilemma shared by most housewives and mothers! We can no more reject these calls than Jesus rejected the harrassment of the multitude. But like Him we should be wise enough to row across the lake—to withdraw from inordinate demands before returning to give ourselves again.

Many ministers work under stress of one kind or another. In this they are not unique; every profession has its forms of stress, and in medicine, politics and the stage, for instance, these are fairly obvious. The fact that the Presbyterian minister is his own master is itself a stress-factor. It means that he has to order his time, to establish priorities in his work, and to decide how hard to drive himself and when to apply the brakes. Our own master? But that is only true in human terms. We are servants of Christ, under-shepherds if you like, and so long as we are conscious of this and responsive to His Spirit the pressure will not break us. We will not just react to the world and its demands, and our priorities will sort themselves out.

Even so, we have a number of peculiar difficulties to contend with. The doctor has evidence that his ministrations are successful; but we can only hope and pray that ours are so. The doctor is expected to have medical skills, but as a man he is accepted for what he is; but many people have false expectations of what we should be, and do not accept us for what we are. We are given a role to play, a mask to wear, and unless we conform some are disappointed in us.

You should not have to wear a mask. Yet when what is expected of you is that you should always be courteous and kind, appreciative and encouraging, cheerful and willing, you know that these are expectations which you yourself would share; but with which you find it difficult always to comply: and there is again a degree of tension.

However full our days, they contain much apparently wasted effort. It is a profession in which one is very conscious of opportunities missed and things left undone.

To 'forget the things that are behind and press on' is the only sensible course. Moreover to worry about the future—a difficult meeting, perhaps, or a special service, is as futile as to repine the past. 'Take no thought for the morrow: sufficient unto the day...' that is, live in the present. More than anything else this reduces stress.

Visiting is full of frustrations. Not untypical was this experience of my wife's. When she came in one day at five o'clock I asked, 'How did it go?' 'Pretty frustrating,' she said; 'since two o'clock I've only seen two-and-a-half.' 'How come?' 'Well, I started at the Infirmary, and the man had gone home. Then I saw someone else there, but I had to kick my heels for twenty minutes in the waiting room first. Then, at the next hospital the woman wasn't in the ward. I tracked her down, eventually, in the grounds walking with two friends who didn't go away, so that was half a visit! Then across to Broomhouse. A top flat and a ground floor, but both out. And last, to an old lady in a top flat. She was out, so I saw her neighbour and left a message. But I'd just got into the car when Mrs Smith appeared, so I went back with her and she had to put the kettle on so that was a long one. Not much done!'

Many an afternoon is like that. One can only take it philosophically, and remember that the card you left has told someone they are not forgotten.

Elijah symbolises the loneliness of the prophets. This is a burden which, to a lesser degree, we share. Because you work unsocial hours, because you are a leader and trying to keep ahead, and because you cannot give yourself in the deepest of friendships to any one person in the congregation but can only maintain a lesser level of friendship with many, you experience isolation. Your very thinking, coloured by the theological uncertainties of the age, and by current dubiety about the institutional Church, may prove a barrier.

When the shoe pinches in all these places and one feels guilt at one's failure to cope, there is a real danger, unless one has the humility to look for help and the spiritual resourcefulness to find it, of becoming a burnt-out case.

Best of all is the therapy of the Sacrament, provided for this very purpose of forgiveness and renewal.

111

Marriage problems

If a husband and wife who are pursuing seemingly irreconcilable careers were to go to a marriage guidance counsellor he would in his wisdom try to make them see the possibility of compromise. Could *he* not agree to give more time to his wife; and *she* to participate more in the life of the parish? But such advice, I believe, would come better from a fellow minister. I, for instance, can say that I fully appreciate the husband's dilemma; his love for his wife and yet his resolve to be true to his vocation; his 'marriage' to his congregation and responsibility before God for his parish. But what I would tell him is this. A married man has obligations to his wife however high and holy his work may be; and it is not impossible to fulfil the one without neglecting the other. You should so order your days that by Friday your Sunday preparation is 'in the bag'; then you will be able to lay it aside and give much of Saturday, or even Friday evening to your family. (Friday is the worst night for visiting, in any case, as many make it their night out. And though it is a popular night for youth organisations, the brief, unexpected visit there by the minister is no less effective than his constant attendance.)

Moreover if for the sake of wife and family, the minister sets out later, or returns earlier from a normal evening's work (apart from those given to committees which may be interminable!) little harm will be done. If it takes you two years rather than one to get round the congregation, how much does it matter? After all, you will probably be there a long time, and what you did not achieve yesterday you will remedy tomorrow.

A minor but not insignificant problem concerns entertaining. In simpler days it was taken for granted that the manse had an open door, and that one of its functions was to be a hostel and a meeting-place for all and sundry. There are still parishes where, in spite of the stringencies of modern life, this is to be found. But things have changed. When as a student I went to address a Bible Class in a country town, I was given a lavish lunch at the manse along with about a dozen other guests—the schoolmaster, the organist and several church members, with their wives. That does not happen today. Not only is it too costly, but most ministers' wives have neither time nor energy to lay it on.

Most manses do what they can, and entertain in a small way. There are unreasonable husbands who expect their wives to be constant hostesses, and wives who feel no obligations except towards their friends. But in many manses there is an unease of conscience about it:

should we not be doing more? Each must judge for himself; but surely it is a balance between too much and nothing at all.

Loneliness

Loneliness can be a major problem. In remote parts of the country, in areas of cultural deprivation, and in some where the character of the people is phlegmatic or 'dour' a minister who has been raised in a very different environment can feel isolated. Regrettably there are Presbyteries whose members meet only superficially and infrequently, for business, and fail to give mutual support or provide real fellowship.

In urban parishes loneliness takes other forms. The conscientious pastor in a vast housing estate, like the busy doctor, has little time to cultivate his peers. In the medical profession this is probably a main cause of the acknowledged high incidence of breakdown, alcoholism and drug addiction. The minister can be advised to join a fraternal or any similar group that is available; but he may well reply that he has not the time. In which case I can only again regret our repudiation of the pastoral Bishop.

The ministry of a woman is essentially no different from that of a man. But the proportion of unmarried women in the ministry is greater than that of unmarried men. To bear the burdens of a parish alone, while looking after oneself in a family-size house, and at the same time establishing oneself in a hitherto male profession, may cause considerable stress. When she is married and a mother, the domestic responsibilities of the woman minister will also exceed those of her male colleagues. She may also have to suffer the attitudes of those, both in parish and presbytery, who still cannot accept the ministry of women; and, cut off from others who are undergoing the same experience, feel desperately alone. And, though one hopes this is temporary, the kinds of parish at present open to her are apt to contain the lowest ratio of 'support persons' in terms of leadership and training. Only time, understanding from her male colleagues, and above all an unwavering sense of vocation will carry her through. No, not only these: both for men and women the love of one's vocation is the best remedy of all.

23 Time to Breathe

By now you may well be asking, Who is sufficient for these things? That I have carried out all the advice I have given is far from being the case. In the first place, I would not have had the stamina, physical and mental, let alone spiritual, to compass adequately all these facets of the parish ministry. In the second, my own ministry has borne too poor a resemblance to that which I have delineated. How often have I botched the worship, maundered on in the sermon, and given it without pause in a high-pitched voice; chosen the wrong hymns; prayed without being prayerful; failed to give helpful counsel or to pray where prayer was needed; neglected organisations and leaders; and missed opportunities of outreach, inter-church cooperation and community action. None of us is sufficient; but 'He who calls you is faithful and he will do it...' (1 Thess 5.24)

If we are to find a satisfying *modus vivendi*, as well as a *modus operandi*, we must get our feet on the ground. You can be big-hearted without saying yes to every request, or attending every meeting (I have heard of ministers who attend, unnecessarily, every meeting of the Guild!), or serving on every committee, or letting every caller sit as long as he should please. Nor are you obliged to read every word of the 'bumph' which accumulates on your desk.

You can clear away impedimenta. You can delete days from your diary. You can say 'I'm sorry, but I can't take the wedding, or attend the committee then: I shall be on holiday.' Or, 'If you don't mind, I won't join the bowling club. I'd like to look in sometimes; but the garden is all I can manage in the summer.'

Apart from formal engagements and the Sunday deadline, the minister's time is paradoxically both far from being his own, and is his own to regulate. There is a pile of work to which I am committed, things to write, people to see, books and papers to read, thinking, planning and praying to be done—but when, and for how long? Without self-discipline I may veer to one extreme or the other; either fritter time away or, and this is more likely, become a 'workaholic' incapable of calling a halt. The inability to relax is a sin, and we should see it as such.

As for your wife, it is not enough that she should share in the life of the congregation and the cares of the parish. To spend and be spent together in the service of God is a precious thing. But there are other joys which you should not withhold from her. Every wife wants to be taken out from time to time by her husband; away from the sphere of work for a trip in the car, a meal out, a visit to friends, a shopping expedition or even—and some manse couples never know this—an evening together by the fire. How longsuffering, too, are those wives whose husbands insist on unwinding every Monday on the golf course with fellow-ministers.

A more serious loss than that of inspiration is that of vision. Many a great text which we give our people for their comfort, we should take also to ourselves—in this instance Habakkuk's 'If the vision tarries, wait for it: it will surely come.'

And we need proper holidays; interludes from the unremitting pressure of professional obligations. To get away from it all.

24 A Charge to Keep

Unless we continue on our own spiritual pilgrimage our ministry will be without contagion and uncreative. Whether we pray regularly and at set times or not, we should strive to live always in the sense of God's presence. It is one of the blessings of our profession that the very nature of our work helps us to do this; that dealing day by day with holy things our hearts and minds are oriented towards God. The converse being the danger that familiarity with it all will breed professionalism and superficiality.

To avert this, we need constantly to remind ourselves of the nature of our calling; in Charles Wesley's words that

A Charge to keep I have,
A God to glorify.

And as we prepare and lead the worship; dispense the sacraments and instruct the young; visit the sick and lonely and comfort those in trouble; and are deeply involved in the life of church and parish, our own faith is constantly renewed. Our preaching, too, when it is 'in the Spirit' is a colloquy with God.

'To whom much is given...' The much that is required of us is not in terms of effort and energy which are self-consuming, but of openness towards God and man. And our prayer should be the one expressed by an unknown servant of Christ more than four hundred years ago; for then, as now, life could be crammed with consuming demands.

Lord temper with tranquillity
Our manifold activity
That we may do our work for Thee
With very great simplicity.

The arrow prayers that we utter on many a doorstep or as we ascend the pulpit, the unassuming, unassertive ways in which we minister, following the pattern of the Beatitudes, and our dependence on spiritual resources, will all procure this end.

To equip yourself it is not enough to acquire the knowledge and follow the advice contained in these pages. You have also to seek God's glory, wherever it is to be found; through the lives of saints and in saints alive; through the beauty of holiness and the holiness of beauty; through music and silence; through human love and the love that is 'beyond all loves excelling'; through the sacramental universe and the Church's sacraments; through the glory that is in all sacrifice and in the one true perfect sacrifice of the Cross.